Donald Macpherson
7 Meikle Gardens
Westhill
Aberdeenshire

Bought at the Portsoy
Boat Festival
2nd July 2011

The Trout and Sea Trout Rivers of Scotland

The Trout and Sea Trout Rivers of Scotland

Roderick Wilkinson

SWAN HILL
PRESS

Copyright © Roderick Wilkinson, 1990

This edition first published in 1990
by Swan Hill Press, an imprint of
Airlife Publishing Ltd

British Library Cataloguing in Publication Data

Wilkinson, Roderick
  The trout and sea trout rivers of Scotland.
  1. Scotland. Trout. Angling
  I. Title
  799.1′755′09411

  ISBN 1-85310-094-4

Swan Hill Press

An imprint of Airlife Publishing Ltd
101 Longden Road, Shrewsbury SY3 9EB, England

Contents

Acknowledgements

I would like to thank the many people in Scotland who helped me in all sorts of ways to write this book. Among these are:–

The staff on Level Four of the Glasgow Mitchell Library who gave me helpful access to the hundreds of angling books ancient and modern.

The Directors of the various Regional Tourist Boards who sent me current information on angling facilities in their area.

The secretaries of the many angling clubs and associations who answered patiently my many questions.

The owners and managers of fishing hotels.

The fishing-tackle shop owners, and in particular Jim Kent of Yoker, Glasgow.

Dr Richard Shelton and Mr Andrew Walker of the Freshwater Fish Laboratory at Faskally, Perthshire.

Mr David MacKay, Deputy Director of the Clyde River Purification Board.

Mr Wm Miller, Chairman of the Upper Clyde Angling Protection Association Ltd.

Mr Drew Jamieson, Director of Water Recreation Services, Lothian Regional Council.

Mr Douglas Nicholson, devoted angler and good friend.

Mr Alex Fraser of Forres for his pictures of the Findhorn.

Photographic Credits

Scotland's river trout

There is a peculiar idea held by some anglers in Scotland that the brown trout really belongs to the lochs of this small, mountainous land and that they are merely tolerated — sometimes as nuisances — in the rivers. Indeed, above the Highland line, the term 'a fish' refers only to one kind of fish — the salmon. Anything else in the rivers is ignored or got rid of.

Of course, in some instances there are reasons for this attitude. As one ghillie put it to me recently, on the banks of the Naver in Sutherland, 'Now just think about it for a minute. What angler who has just paid a thousand pounds for a week's fishing in this river is going to be the least bit interested in trout fishing?'

'All that's quite true, but tell me this — are the brown trout there?'

'Thousands of them.'

'Who fishes for them?'

'Nobody. There's only one kind of fish up here — and that's the salmon.'

Another reason given by the anti-trout people is that trout are fierce competitors for food with immature salmon and will even consume small parr, thus reducing future salmon stocks. Frankly, this notion hardly bears up when we consider the Tweed (to mention only one famous salmon river) where excellent trout as well as many other kinds of fish thrive together.

Happily there are many factors which will gladden the hearts of dedicated trout anglers in Scotland. Rivers like the Clyde, which are not particularly famed for the quality of their salmon fishing, support excellent trout fishing. As I have mentioned in the case of the Tweed, some famous salmon rivers also have good trout fishing. And some rivers like the Spey have as great a reputation for their sea trout as for their salmon. So the scene is a glorious mixter-maxter which only requires to be sorted out for the benefit of those fishers who favour trout and sea trout angling in Scotland's rivers.

Much of the trout fishing in Scotland's salmon rivers is managed by local angling clubs who allow visitors to fish for very moderate charges. However, the development of strong carbon-fibre rods, used in conjunction with weighted flies and lead-cored lines, has been causing many riparian owners to rub their chins dubiously. Who is to say that the trout angler with such equipment is *not* trying for a salmon? The use of spinning gear when the water level is of the appropriate height, makes for a confused angling scene on some rivers. The best answer I feel is a 'combined' ticket for association or club waters that permits fishing for salmon, sea trout or brown trout, as they have on the Spey at Grantown or Boat of Garten.

For all this, there are many rivers in Scotland which are a delight for trout or sea trout fishing. I have fished for years on the upper reached of that Solway river, the Annan, around Johnstonbridge or Wamphrey, and have enjoyed every sylvan hour. And the Border Esk around Canonby has great runs of sea trout in the summer; likewise the North Esk near Montrose and the Ythan estuary at Newburgh. The brown trout of the Clyde are famed all over Scotland and the association members of the Tweed downstream from Peebles would hardly thank you for any other kind of fishing than for trout.

Although it would be a wiser angler than I to strike a difference in the pleasure or challenge between salmon and trout fishing, I do have an opinion. Certainly, like most others who have hunted the salmon, I have spotted my fish, tied on what I believed to be exactly the correct fly, cast over him and hooked him. Of course I have. Having said that, I am under no doubt that many of the other salmon I have taken were 'shots in the dark' — caught, of course, at the most likely spot and with what I felt was the right fly or lure at the right time; but they were shots in the dark nevertheless. And I would be amazed if our most expert salmon anglers could swear that every fish caught was the one they spotted and the one for which they cast a fly. There is a lot of chuck-it-and-chance-it about salmon angling, though only the trollers in Loch Tay might admit it.

This is not to say that there is no wild guessing about trout or sea trout fishing. Of course there is. But I feel the element of chuck-

The author ready for a day's challenge.

it-and-chance-it is less. And in the case of dry-fly fishing upstream (or, for that matter, clear-water worming), there is not much scope for chucking it or for chancing it. It is the true angler's art to spot the tell-tale circles made by a feeding trout and to cast the single fly over him so that he is deceived and caught.

For as long as angling has been known as the gentle art, this form of trout fishing has been hallowed and perfected in the chalk streams of England. In the Test, the Kennet or the Itchen, to mention only three, any other type of fishing in unthinkable. In the more northern parts of England, and certainly in Scotland, upstream dry flying, too, is a highly respected method but with this difference — the rivers, generally, are more oxygenated necessitating 'white water' fishing. This means that the dry flyers who come to fish a river in Scotland have the added challenge of 'reading' the turbulent parts of the water where the trout are lying behind rocks, or in the calmer streams, to feed with minimum effort on the insects carried downstream.

Wet-fly fishing downstream, however, still seems to be the most popular method of river fishing in Scotland. This is evident when a visiting angler walks into a tackle shop to buy artificial flies for the local river. He will usually be offered a selection of wet flies like Green-well's Glory, Butcher, Grouse or Claret and in many cases a made-up cast of three flies ready for use.

It would be a brave writer who tried to persuade his readers that brown trout fishing on rivers in Scotland is more enjoyable or fruitful than on lochs. Each to his taste. I know many loch anglers who have never cast a fly on a river and vice versa. But for those who just want a good day's fishing on a river, here are some things to consider.

Every step along the river bank reveals a fresh opportunity for a cast. The river scene changes at every bend and the angler really uncovers his own challenge by choosing where he will fish. Unlike a loch, a river and the fish in it reflect the changes in rainfall, light, shade and, of course, the time of day. (The one element which affects the loch and not the river is the wind.) All these things indicate to the angler the size and type of fly he will use, where he will wade, where he will stand, how far he will cast and exactly where he should place his flies. They will even indicate, if he fishes, for instance, in the deep sunset, what size of trout he might catch.

So far as surroundings and scenery are concerned, there are no generalities I can offer about Scotland's lochs versus its rivers. The River Leven in Dumbartonshire brings salmon and sea trout by the thousands from the Firth of Clyde through an industrial area which could hardly be described, even by the locals, as the best of Scottish scenery. Yet the loch at the start of the river to which these fish are heading, is the wonderful and beautiful Loch Lomond along whose 'bonny bonnie banks' tourists travel in breathless admiration.

There are no hard and fast guidelines. I have fished in some dreary, uninteresting lochs and reservoirs and I have also cast a line in some of the loveliest rivers in Europe — all in Scotland and sometimes within a few miles.

One generality I *can* offer, however, is that fishing for trout or sea trout in Scotland's rivers is a challenging and exhilarating experience for any angler. And the fish are there to be caught — thousands of them every year.

How we catch trout in Scotland

Generally speaking, we angle for fish here in Scotland very much as they do in other countries. We fly-fish, we spin, or we use bait.

Most of the anglers I have met on river banks catch their trout by any of these methods:

Dry-fly fishing casting upstream

Some say this is the only sportsman-like way to fish for trout or even sea trout on Scottish rivers; the single fly is fished across the river or upstream. Apart from ethical considerations, the method is more satisfying, more of an 'art' and, when performed by an expert, it is a more effective way of catching more and bigger fish.

Wet-fly fishing downstream

In terms of sportsmanship, this is next in line — in the opinion of many anglers. It is my favourite method although I catch less and possibly smaller fish than my dry-fly companions. In some conditions there is an element of chuck-it-and-chance-it, though some fishers would hotly deny this.

Worm(s) fished downstream in spate water

Yes, I have enjoyed fishing downstream in a big water with the Brandling striped worm, especially when the water is running yellow or brown. Contrary to what most people might think, the method requires skill in defining accurately how the nylon leader is to be weighted to reach the precise depth where the fish may be. Another skill is in coaxing the bait from the main current into the bank in a natural fashion. That is where the fish are usually lying in heavy water — just where you would lie if you were a fish; all they have to do is ease out of the quieter water now and then to snatch a passing worm, preferably the angler's.

Worm(s) fished upstream in clear water

For all that some angling experts write about the skill and technique required for upstream clear-water worming, it is not my favourite way of catching trout on a river. The best experiences I have had were on the little hill burns 'stalking' fish, crouching down out of the skyline and delicately fishing a single worm upstream into the turbulence of a waterfall, or a well-shaded, deep, pool caused by the tumbling water above it.

The Mayfly (in its season) fished upstream

The only time I have fished with this insect was on Elvan Water, a tributary of the Clyde. And the results were excellent. In the short Mayfly season, trout go mad for it and will feed on nothing else.

The 'gadger' (stone-insect) or grub fished downstream

On the Clyde again, this time near Roberton, I have had some grand fishing with the little white grub obtained from inside the stem of a dock leaf. In near darkness, it caught many trout.

The fly-and-maggot fished in the evening

This is a method which always fascinated me when I saw anglers practising it. So I tried it a few times on a Border river when fishing for sea trout. I caught some sizeable finnock but I never use the method now, simply because I have never found a way of getting the wretched maggot to stay on the tail fly!

Spinning with a Mepp spoon, or a small Toby spoon

Spinning for trout? Not for me. To my mind an angler has to be rather desperate for a fish to use this method — although I have caught sea trout up to 3 lb in weight with a small spoon in fast-moving water. And I have used the spinner with a Thomson spoon when fishing for big river rainbow trout in Canada.

There are two main schools of thought about fly fishing in Scotland and their adherents are poles apart. The first school's views are expressed by a well-known Scottish angling author who says he contents himself with no more than three patterns of flies, one of them a Greenwell's Glory. He uses them all the time on hill and moorland lochs in the far north. And he is quite satisfied with his catching record.

The second school is reflected in the two books written by the late Bert Sharp who, for forty years' was an acknowledged expert on many lowland rivers. His first book, *Let's fish Clyde*, and the second one, *Let's fish again*, are, in my opinion, masterpieces on Scottish fly patterns, how to tie them and how to fish with them. His precision of description, supported by his own experiences with various flies and nymphs on Scottish river waters, is quite remarkable. What is more important, he was a formidable and highly respected fish catcher.

For my part, I have had experience in both schools and have tried all sorts of sizes and patterns on many rivers. In very general terms, I have made some conclusions:

1. When fishing the Clyde and its many tributaries, from the Daer down through Camps, Powtrail and Duneaton Waters as far as Lamington, I have never caught trout with any fly unless it was slightly tatty, sparsely dressed and dingey-grey or black — certainly without colour.

2. Conversely, a few miles across the hill on the Annan at Wamphrey, the trout will go for colourful flies like Cinnamon-and-gold or Grouse and Claret. And, of course, Greenwell's.

3. Fishing for trout downstream wet on the Tweed has, for me, often been a very frustrating experience. Why? Because up around Peebles, you cannot afford to make mistakes about the flies on which the fish are feeding on a particular day. It seems to me that Tweed trout are the choosiest in the world and will disdain anything which does not resemble just what is hatching at that time. And this applies to both wet and dry flies.

4. There are days in the early summer on the Tay when trout behave like those on the Tweed. Favourite Tay patterns can be cast at them all day while the trout are clearly feeding in every pool, and they will ignore them. Then, just as the flies are changed for the umpteenth — and last — time, trout are caught. You have cracked it! On such days, usually a Teal and Green did the trick.

5. I have found the famous Loch Leven 'wee doubles' very effective when fishing for finnock in the estuary of the Spey. Different patterns from the Loch Leven favourites, of course. Finnock on the Spey like colour and glitter, as they do on the Findhorn near Forres.

For all these generalities, based on my own experiences, I do feel that every river has its own 'trick'. The aim of a river trouter in Scotland should be to find out as quickly as possible the eccentricities of the trout or the sea trout on a particular river. The way to do this is to watch the locals, ask them, ask the local tacklist, then do as others do. After all, the local anglers have generations of inherent knowledge about fishing 'their' river. And you will never learn any of it unless you watch, ask and listen.

The river trouter in Scotland

What is a trout river? Is it a trout river if it also contains salmon? Is it a trout river if sea trout run up it to spawn? Is it a trout river if all the trout have been killed off by pollution or neglect? Is it still a trout river if the salmon have virtually taken over? And what about grayling and coarse fish?

The description seems easier to define in England than in Scotland, particularly in the south where rivers like the Itchen, the Test and the Kennet, are famed predominantly for the excellence of their trout fishing. In Scotland the whole angling sport on a river can be a blend of salmon, grilse, trout, grayling, sea trout, finnock and even coarse fish, each in the prime of their season. This is not the result of any particular disorder, either by man or nature; rather is it the result of an abundance of excellent fishing of all kinds in a land of rushing torrents and unpolluted streams.

Notwithstanding this happy accident of plenty in such a small country, there are waters which can be properly called trout rivers. The Tweed is certainly one, even though it is better known for its salmon; and the coarse fishing around Kelso is among the best in Britain. The Aberdeenshire Don is another; its salmon fishing is improving every year now that the pollution in the lower reaches is under better control. Some salmon rivers have sea trout runs of such proficiency that it would be a disservice to omit them from my description of a trout river. I imagine that the anglers of the Border Esk or the Ythan in Aberdeenshire might have a justifiable complaint if their waters were ignored.

'Up where the trout lies dreaming . . .'

Add to this glorious mixter-maxter the fact that rivers change in character. The Clyde, that busy waterway through the city of Glasgow that was a midwife to the Industrial Revolution, the cradle of the world's shipbuilding, oozy, grimy, weed-ribboned, and utterly polluted for over a century, is now once again — believe it or not — a salmon river. Most of this particular success has been due to the work of the Clyde River Purification Board, among other bodies. Salmon are now regularly sighted from the banks as far upstream as Rutherglen, a Clyde-side burgh of busy streets and houses.

The Forth, too, is slowly but surely winning the battle against pollution (to say nothing of poaching and illegal netting). Again, that river's Purification Board is proving to be a good friend of the angler.

It would be almost impossible to list and describe every single river, stream and burn which contains trout or sea trout. Most pools in virtually every stream that is a tributary of one of Scotland's main rivers have trout in them — either as residents or as migrating sea trout. Some in the remote mountain or wilderness areas are of little interest to trout anglers, either because getting to them is almost impossible for the ordinary angler or there are other hindrances to access.

In spite of the confusion of waters and the types of fish in them, whether the waters are managed and when they may be fished, some generalities *can* be made about trout fishing in Scotland.

Angling for brown trout (or its non-migrating brothers like the American brook trout) is a more popular activity on the hundreds of lochs, usually from a boat but sometimes from the bank. In mountainous or moorland areas and certainly in the streams that run through peaty or acidic soil, trout are smaller, rarely exceeding ½ lb. In the better nourished areas, especially those with a limestone base, trout are bigger. No simple geographical line can be drawn to clarify boundaries. While it might be convenient to say that trout in Highland streams are smaller than those farther south, this is not the case. The limestone-based lochs in the far north prove the contrary by the size of the trout caught.

One myth about trout fishing in Scotland — that is free and unfettered — can be destroyed. It is nothing of the kind. Every piece of water,

loch or river, is owned or managed by someone. And a permit to fish is required before setting up a rod and line. For trout fishing the charge is usually very low and in some cases absurdly cheap. Sea trout permits usually go with those for salmon and are, therefore, more expensive.

The visiting angler who wants to fish in an area has three choices in finding out where to go and how to get a permit. First, he can simply write to the tourist office of the district and they will send him a leaflet describing the various fishing waters and where he may get permission to fish. In some of the really popular fishing places — like Tayside or the Scottish borders embracing the Tweed — tourist offices charge a small fee for an excellent booklet giving plenty of detail and even including the artificial flies recommended for certain rivers.

Second, he can book into one of the many fishing hotels that advertise in angling magazines. Most of these hotels, for example on Speyside, provide permits from the local angling association, and others have their own private stretches of river. Some run fishing schools and give tuition for the entire family.

Third, he can go to the local fishing tackle shop in a town or village and make enquiries. Most tacklists sell permits for their local waters and one of the advantages of this method is that the angler is given personal advice. However, it should be remembered that the tacklist is not mainly in the advice business. He is selling fishing tackle!

Let us leave the salmon anglers to their expensive beats and consider the various types of enthusiasts who love fishing for trout and sea trout on Scotland's rivers, from springtime till the golden leaves of autumn are speckling the waters.

There are the Scottish anglers themselves; most are members of local clubs and associations; most are evening or Saturday anglers; and most of them fish fairly, considerately and skilfully. Few return home with an empty creel.

There are the holiday visitors and tourists staying in hotels, rented cottages, caravans and on camp sites, or as guests of friends. Many of them are anglers who packed a rod in the hope of finding a fishing spot on a river. Some are simply fathers who want to introduce members of their families to the 'gentle art' on a Scottish river.

Then there are the experts. They come to Scotland virtually from all over the world to fish the waters. The better off pay exalted prices for the famous beats; the others do not. Among the latter is a growing number of fanatics whose summer vacation time more closely relates to the sea trout runs on certain rivers than the autumn salmon runs on others.

There is another group — the ordinary angler like you and me who just wants a few days quiet fishing on a good stream and who is more interested in fishing than fish!

In praise of the river trouter

He stalks his quarry. He is a hunter. He is also a philosopher, something of a poet, a deceiver, an artificer and, at times, a liar. He is not a meat hunter. He is a trout angler.

When it comes to fishing, comparisons are odious. Who is to say that the coarse fishers lining the banks of canals and sluggish rivers in the Midlands of England are any less noble in their sport than the big river men in chest waders who wield 16-foot rods on the Royal Dee? The ruddy-faced, cheerful aficionados who go out to sea with their mates in chartered boats, deserve as good a salute to their dexterity with their pirks and cocktail baits as the long-lining rainbow trout fanatics who heave their lures into the stocked, still waters with weight-forward lines. Fishing's fishing.

Of course, I am prejudiced. I like trout anglers. And when I meet them on a river I like them more. Three men in a boat on a loch, one on the oars and the other two thrashing the water for hours is not my idea of an ideal day's fishing, especially on blank days. Of course, most of the statistics are against me; they catch more fish, etcetera, etcetera. But that, let me suggest, is not the object of the exercise. There are all sorts of ways to catch trout, particularly on a loch. You can troll, dap, use sunk lures, jiggle worms — even net them. What is

important is the fishing — not the fish.

I hope you agree. If you do, read on. If not, please content yourself with this morning's price of fish at Aberdeen fish market.

There was a time in Britain when the whole sport had only two classes. You fished for salmon if you were gentry; you fished for trout otherwise. Today, by and large, it is much the same though the edges are more blurred and 'money' has replaced the 'gentry' syndrome.

One of the dimensions where it is blurred is in the world of the sea trout. The season is a short one (in most rivers not more than about ten weeks) and the type of angler who goes after them is as wily, as cunning and as patient as the fish. Like the salmon, the sea trout is a fish of the sea, migrating up river to spawn, but unlike the salmon it feeds voraciously on its journey. It is often found lurking in dark places under banks shaded by overhanging bushes and trees. And the people who go after them fish during the purple sunset for those shadowy big ones, or venture into the roaring, white waters in the daytime. They are trout anglers supreme and their skill on rivers and estuaries is unique and specific. This is why I esteem them as much as brown trout anglers.

There is a lot to be said in favour of fishing for trout on rivers — even on those waters that are world-famous for their salmon. Certainly it is less expensive. Over £1,000 for a week in the prime season is not unusual on a salmon river and can hardly be compared to a daily or weekly ticket for trout fishing costing a few pounds. Fishing for trout is not so dependent on weather conditions as for salmon. And the best season for good trouting is usually longer than the prime time for salmon.

Not all anglers come to Scotland to fish for salmon; many visiting anglers feel more at home with a trout rod. Salmon rivers are scarcer in England than in Scotland and access to them is a very costly business. Trout waters, both rivers and lakes, are more common, thus lighter on the angler's pocket. This means that more anglers in England handle a trout rod than a salmon one.

Then there are the young people. Big time salmon is a sport that, mainly because of its high cost, is the privilege of grown-ups, more men than women. It is very unusual to see a boy or girl using a salmon rod. For a youngster, trout fishing with rod and line on a river has a

Fishing for sea trout in the gloaming on a Solway river.

fitness-to-purpose feel about it, particularly when fishing with dad.

The earliest record on the art of fly fishing is a treatise written by an abbess, no less, in which she explains how to tie artificial flies around a concealed hook and how to catch trout with them. She was writing about river trout — no mention of lakes, or lochs, or reservoirs. Nor do I have any recollection of Izaak Walton explaining in his writings about fishing on still waters. Of course in the days of the abbess and later in *The Compleat Angler*, they cast their lines for the natural inhabitants of the river. Today's stocking policies by the many clubs and associations on rivers means that there are more fish, bigger fish and more sport for more anglers.

There is something about 'waiting for the rise' that brings out the very best in fishing for trout on a river. Sometimes there is another angler to sit beside and to share a flask of coffee and to tell about the one that got away farther upstream. More often you are alone with the birds, the occasional passing butterfly and the dappled sun pattern on the babbling water shining through the trees on the far bank. Then you see the rise . . . a dimpling causing a ring on the gently gliding pool as it drifts downstream: then another, this time nearer the far bank, signifying a good-size fish. You screw the top on your flask, put it softly in your haversack, rise slowly and, as quietly as possible, walk to the water, peel off line from your reel, make a few false casts to get the distance right . . . then make *the* cast and watch your flies lightly kiss the water then drift downstream as they submerge.

You stand stock-still, holding your breath. You have the distance right. Your tail fly is the right one. Your nylon leader does not drag.

Bang!

The fish is on. The line straightens out as you see the swirl under the trees and you gently raise the rod, setting the hook. The rod bends. A good fish – a big fish. The trout dashes all over the pool as you hold the rod up, up . . . a few minutes later he is in the net.

Of course I go fishing in lochs and reservoirs. Of course I fish in the sea from rocks or when out in a boat with cheery mates. And of course I have many blank days on my favourite rivers. But it is those other days on a good trout river that make living worth while.

Those I have loved . . .

I would be surprised if anyone except Her Majesty's Royal Engineers had counted, let alone described, every river and stream in Scotland. Running waters of every size and type are countless in this small country of mountains, glens and moors, most of them in areas of wilderness. I would even be more surprised to hear of an angler who had fished all of them.

Of course we know the famous ones and the big ones and the beautiful ones. The Royal Dee, the mighty Tay and the glorious Tweed are world-famous, even among those unfortunate people who do not fish. We also know the mighty Clyde, reverberating with yesterday's shipbuilding cacophony, and the Forth over which spans that famous bridge outside Edinburgh. But I wonder if even enthusiastic anglers know much about the Elvan, or the Ugie, or the Allan Water.

I would love to be able to say that I have fished them all, the big and the small. It would be a delight to describe to my open-mouthed angling friends the skill needed to side-caste for sea trout under trees at night on the Devon, or how to keep a balance on the slippery rocks of the Dochart while fishing for trout, or how to get a permit to fish the Almond if you are not a resident in the district around Perth. Nothing would give me greater pleasure than to boast of sylvan spring days on Tweed-dale burns, or of lilac-coloured summer evenings fishing for herling on the Fleet near Dornoch. Of course, there is hardly a rod and line angler who has not had his day of glory on the Tay, on the Tweed, or on the Spey. With some of us it has been no more than that — an occasional day. For others, it has been an entire week on Tulchan, or on Lower Floors or when dapping Loch Maree.

Some expert, indeed legendary, anglers have fished contentedly on one river all their lives; they have no wish to go elsewhere. Others have spent all their fishing days on one *part* of a river and have never travelled downstream by as much as two miles. For most of us, experience of a dozen waters has satisfied us, fish or no fish. For my part, living and fishing in such a

The River Earn in the heart of Perthshire.

small country as Scotland has given me an opportunity to cast a rod on scores of waters, some for brief periods and others for entire holidays. This parochial activity has been enlivened now and then with fishing trips to America, Canada, Denmark and other far-off places. If nothing else, these trips have served to give me an opinion that Scotland has the most varied and interesting fishing at the lowest cost in the world. The fancy brochures sent out by tourist offices in other countries do not tell us of the distances to be travelled to reach the best fishing waters. Nor do they tell us about the bears, the mosquitoes, the necessity of guides and what they cost, or about the difficulties in obtaining permits. The impression an angler gets too often from these brochures is that the fishing waters are easily accessible, the cost affordable and the natives friendly.

This is not to say that Scotland is blameless

in this respect. Walk into any hotel — even some described as 'a fishing hotel' — and ask the reception clerk about fishing facilities. He or she will either (a) refer you to Angus who can be found in the bar most evenings after eight, (b) send you to the local tourist office, or (c) tell you that they have run out of the local fishing leaflet.

On the other hand, it is fair to say that the local fishing-tackle shop in nearly every small town or village will see you right with excellent advice, a permit and precisely the flies or lures or bait you need.

This says nothing, of course, for the 'big league'. Expensive fishing on expensive beats at the most expensive time of the year is available to those who can afford exclusivity on such famous rivers as the Spey or the Tweed. But Scotland does have facilities on rivers and lochs to suit every pocket. On some rivers, like the Tay where salmon beats can be expensive, there *are* parts of the same river on which an angler can fish for a few pounds a day or week. In Scotland's fishing waters you get what you pay for.

It is not too difficult for me to remember the striking features of every river I have fished, from the wonderful trouting on the Tweed at Peebles to the two salmon caught in an hour in Perthshire: spring fishing for finnock in the estuary of the South Esk . . . the breathtaking anticipation of casts at Dinnet on the Dee . . . upstream dry flying on the Don at Alford . . . the big sea trout on the Ythan estuary . . . five salmon caught in one day on the Mountblairy Fishing on the Deveron . . . the one salmon in a week on the Findhorn . . . no salmon in a week on the Casseley . . . the upstream casting of a wee Stoat's Tail in the deep, dark pools of the Halladale at Forsinard . . . and those wonderful evenings after trout on the Clyde at Elvanfoot.

I wish I could have fished all waters, particularly those that have been sounding their bells of welcome — the Oykel, the Teviot, the Nairn, the Ness, the Beauly, the Conon and scores more. Perhaps these are delights yet to be tasted.

There may come a time when a second Stoddart will travel the length and breadth of Scotland with a fishing rod and cast his flies on almost every river and stream he meets. When Stoddart did this sort of thing in 1847 he did much more than describe every conceivable angling feature about a river: he caught fish by the score.

The Scottish sea trout — that's something else!

A doctor in Switzerland, who reads my occasional articles in German language fishing magazines, comes to Scotland every year with his two sons to fish. For salmon? No. They are sea trout fanatics and literally search the world for the best sea trout fishing.

I first met them a few years ago in the little fishing hotel at Newburgh on the Aberdeenshire coast where, like me, they were fishing the estuary of the Ythan and, also like me, were going mad with the frustration of blank days. I could hardly blame them. Someone should advise visitors to Scotland about the challenge of fishing for our most desirable, elusive, evasive and tantalizing game fish and tell us how to catch them. Those few days on the Ythan were both delightful and perplexing. Anglers there fish only at the turn of the tide and during these few hours there is a frenzy of activity; sea trout are plopping and thrashing about everywhere in the brackish water. Yet, it seems to me, that only when that turn of tide and the light of a lilac gloaming and the amount of fresh water from the river are in ideal juxtaposition will these fish take the fly. Some locals, like fifteen-year-old Cameron Smith, who comes from Wiltshire and lives in Newburgh because his father works in the area, catches about a hundred sea trout in a season. Farmer John McNicoll catches three and four pounders regularly and the fisheries manager, Eddie Forbes, tells me that ten pounders are not uncommon. A German angler from Frankfurt has been coming to the estuary of the Ythan to fish for ten years. It is possible that the only people who really need advice about sea trout fishing on that river, are the Swiss doctor, his sons and me!

Perhaps he and his family were just unlucky. The following year I met them at Glasgow airport returning to Zurich. They had been fishing the Eichaig in Argyllshire all week and had caught nothing. The doctor complained that the fish entering the river from the Clyde estuary, on their way up to spawn in Lock Eck,

were not stopping in pools anywhere en route; they were making mad dashes upstream all week. Next year he may be flying over to fish the Border Esk or the Annan in June or July and I hope he and his family sleep during the day and fish into the velvet darkness with the right flies.

Is it appropriate to link migrating Scottish sea trout with native brown trout, in terms of angling technique and fishing enjoyment? One is a temporary visitor coming home to mate and give birth; the other is a river resident. Both compete for food. Unlike salmon, which does not feed in fresh water, both sea trout and brown trout feed voraciously, although the time, place and season for catching them slightly differ. The sea trout season is a short one on most rivers and is usually confined to June and July. What is appropriate is the challenge of those 'silver savages' which may be caught by trout flies cast downstream 'wet', although the methods demand greater stealth by the angler and greater skill when he is hooked, because the sea trout has a soft mouth.

The fact that the sea trout is migratory seems to me no reason to incorporate it constantly — and usually very briefly — with writings about Scottish salmon fishing. The sea trout is a Prince of Fish in its own right and, in my opinion, it more properly 'belongs' to the trout angler. This view is particularly valid when considering the shoals of young virgin fish that come up Scottish rivers in late May and June: hundreds are caught, for instance, by trout anglers in the estuary of the South Esk with wee trout double-hooked flies. Taking this opinion further, there is a fish in Scotland called a 'slob trout' which is as near to a sea trout as makes little difference. The flesh is

Opposite: Loch Lomond, Ardlui River Falloch and mountains of Ben Dubhchraig.

quite pink and they are caught in the same river estuaries as its migrating brother. In Orkney they abound in the brackish water on the sea-edge of lochs and go up the lochs to spawn.

Size? I will put no exaggerated claims in writing about the relative weight or dimensions of either fish. The angler can make up his own mind. The record brown trout is one of 19 lb 9 oz caught in Loch Quoich in 1978 by J. A. F. Jackson. The record sea trout exceeds that weight by 7 oz — a fish of 20 lb caught on the Tweed at Peebles in 1983 by G. Leavy. Both were caught in Scotland and both are British records.

Why many anglers in Scotland are turning to trout

The sport of salmon fishing in Scotland is being headlined by various events these days. Some anglers say that, for better or for worse, things will never be the same again.

When commercial fish farming of salmon was first started in the sea lochs around the western coasts some years ago, all kinds of scenarios were drawn up by anglers who saw their sport dramatically affected by the ranching of thousands of fish which were to be marketed on a big scale. The most common of these prophecies was that the price of salmon on the market would drop tremendously and this, in turn, would de-popularise the sport of angling. Then, it was said, the owners of valuable salmon beats on rivers would reduce their rental prices so that the sport would be wide open to suit everyone's pocket.

Nothing of the sort has happened. The prices of both farmed and wild salmon have held up and nothing the ever-growing numbers of fish farmers have done seems to have had the prophesied 'domino' effect. The price of fish seems unimportant.

Another belief was that as the price of farmed salmon steadily decreased, poachers might be driven to work harder, steal more fish and to become more aggressive. Yet another was that the legal commercial netting companies would press the authorities for more netting time in order to maintain their turnover of fish and money.

What *has* been happening to affect Scottish salmon anglers, some of it unexpected, is drawing some long faces. Briefly, much river fishing is now beyond the reach and pocket of many enthusiasts. Certainly there are still weekly ticket association waters on the Spey, the Nith, some all too few parts of the Tweed and the Tay, plus some reasonably priced stretches in smaller rivers. But in general terms the whole sport in the really good waters is becoming more and more expensive as riparian owners, quite understandably, take advantage of an affluent market and increasing demand.

Fishing rivers are changing hands, some for enormous sums. The Naver in Sutherland was recently bought with the estate through which it runs for £2,000,000. And time-share beats like the famous Taymount Fishings on the river Tay are now being sold for many thousands of pounds. The good rivers seem to be 'closing in' and people with a modest pocket can no longer get access to those exclusive waters. Although this has always been the situation to a greater or lesser extent, there is no doubt that salmon angling in Scotland is becoming quite prohibitive.

Netting rights are being bought out by a combination of riparian owners and the Atlantic Salmon Conservation Trust, and this, in turn, is increasing the value and the rental of rod fishing upstream.

These are some of the reasons why more and more anglers are fishing for trout and sea trout. Private stillwater fisheries have been opening up all over Scotland and those owned by public authorities have also been improving their facilities and stock. Happily for trout anglers, not all rivers are 'salmon only' and not all rivers are the exclusive preserve of salmon anglers. To this extent trout fishers still have good access at moderate ticket prices to many of the waters all over the country. There are some waters, like the Earn or the Annan in Dumfries-shire, or the Deveron in the north-east, which have all three kinds of game fish and which give a great deal of pleasure to the river trouter. Even in the early winter months such rivers offer the challenge of the 'winter trout', the grayling.

Today, more than ever, fishing for trout and sea trout in Scotland shows a great potential for the angler, the owners of waters, hoteliers and the tourist industry. There are more of these fish and there are more waters that support them.

The Falls of Rogie on the Black Water in the Conon river scheme.

How much does it cost to fish in Scotland?

Writing generally about prices for permits on fishing rivers is always tricky. Prices can change year by year. They vary greatly according to the reputation and value of the fishing. And there is usually every difference in the world between what an angler pays on a good stretch of a good salmon river and what he might pay on a club or association river to fish for trout. Then, in between, is the question of permission to fish for sea trout which is normally included in a salmon permit. Added to this is the fact that few salmon anglers on an expensive beat of a river will bother about sea trout, let alone his resident brother the brown trout.

Staying with fishing for brown trout on rivers, however, prices for a day or a week's fishing are never much higher than a few pounds. Even on the world-famous Tweed, fishing for trout up river around Peebles, a splendid trouting stretch, costs no more than £3 for a day or £9 for a week and £42 for the whole season. On that same stretch if you wish to fish for salmon, the price is £10 for the day and related prices for other periods.

Where things start getting pricey on the Tweed is farther downstream if you wish to fish for salmon or sea trout — and when you want to do so. On the Traquair beat, a permit will cost £210 to £225, plus VAT, for the week, and the fishing here is not available until 10 October. That is by no means the top of the price league on the Tweed. Beats costing a fortune are not unusual down-river where the salmon and sea trout catches in previous years have been very great.

Is it any wonder that sea trout fishing on these valuable beats is largely ignored by trout anglers in favour of the 'big boys'?

The Tweed is the Tweed, of course, and anyone wishing to fish for salmon and/or sea trout in the best beats at the best time of the season must expect to pay high prices. The demand is always there as it is on the Aberdeen-shire Dee, the Spey and, certainly, on the Tay.

For the moderately-minded angler or visiting holiday-maker, or for the tourist who would just 'like to have a few days on a river', Scotland is abundant in wonderful rivers and lochs. Fishing for brown trout only should cost about £5 or so for the day or perhaps £30 for the week. Certainly not more than £10 per day as is the case on most lochs.

Looking for sea trout waters might bring the angler into the 'salmon league' because both are migrating fish and usually occupy the same water, albeit at different times in the season. Salmon run up rivers usually in the spring or the autumn, but sea trout on most waters conveniently wait until summer for the tourist or holiday angler. While this is advantageous for all concerned, it does not mean that the owners or managers of rivers can make a lot of distinction. In summertime, grilse (virgin salmon coming up for the first time) often join their sea trout cousins. So how is the riparian owner to sell a permit 'for sea trout only'?

There are, nevertheless, scores of rivers in Scotland where fishing for sea trout in the summer months costs about £10 for the day or £50 for the week. Some association waters are lower in price where £3 for a day is not unusual. The best plan for a visiting angler is to enquire in advance from the riparian owner or from the fishing club.

Of course, there is another way to have an excellent fishing holiday for trout or sea trout in Scotland, particularly in summer, and that is to stay at a fishing hotel. Some hotels have waters which they lease exclusively from estate owners. Others simply reach agreement with local associations or clubs for their guests to have permission to fish their waters. Others say they can arrange fishing but do no more than send a guest along to the tackle shop to buy a permit.

This is not to infer that there is anything inferior about a local association water. On Speyside there are well-managed associations who issue permits to anglers staying in the area for seven days or more. The permits are very reasonable at around £30 for the week — and cover salmon, sea trout and trout. The same situation prevails in other areas such as the Nith at Thornhill, or on parts of the Tweed.

The ideal angling holiday is to stay at a

Midsummer on the Endrick, Loch Lomond's main tributary.

fishing hotel that has exclusive rights on a river. In these hotels most of the guests are anglers accompanied by families or friends and there is often a congenial air of competition on each day's outing to the water. The Grant Arms Hotel at Monymusk in Aberdeenshire, or the Richmond Arms Hotel at Tomintoul, are examples of this kind of arrangement.

There is good sports fishing in Scotland to suit everyone's taste and pocket and, in general terms, the angler gets what he pays for.

. . . but when does the fishing season start?

The angling guides say that the trout fishing season in Scotland opens on 15 March and ends on 6 October. And, of course, they are right. It has been a statutory offence to catch brown trout outside these dates for many years.

Then came the boom in stillwater fishing and private fisheries and the introduction of rainbow trout to lakes and reservoirs. Now the opening and closing dates are all over the place. Some rivers and lochs open on 1 April and others end on 30 September. By opening a little later and closing a little earlier, trout have a better opportunity to mature and get the best of the food in the water.

In the case of lochs which are stocked with both rainbow and brown trout, some remain open until the end of October, presumably because rainbows are outside the statutory season. What happens if an angler, fishing in one of these lochs, catches a brown trout after the official closing date for that fish? Frankly, he should release the fish back into the water because (a) to keep it is illegal, (b) it is better for the fish, its feeding and breeding, and (c) the chances are that the trout may not be in the best condition for the table.

The season for salmon fishing, of course, has

Fishing for sea trout on the estuary of the Fleet near Dornoch.

always been all over the place, and for a good reason — the salmon, as a migrating fish, ascends our rivers all year round. The main run of these fish, however, differs from one river to another and this is the prime consideration of a district's salmon fishing board when it lays down the opening and closing dates for both commercial netting and sports fishing by rod and line. A salmon river can only support a certain number of migrating fish and a balance must be struck between this factor and the requirements of netters and anglers.

The earliest salmon rivers to open their season are those in the north of Scotland, some as early as January. Farther south, the first to open is the Tay on 15 January. Some close at the end of September, others in October. The Tweed and the Nith close as late as the end of November. Thus, these two rivers are closed for salmon angling for only two months in the year.

What about sea trout? The variance in stocks of these fish, between one river and another, depends on when shoals come upstream. As a very general rule, on most rivers, the best time to fish for them is in the early part of summer — May, June and early in July. Local hoteliers, river owners, and keepers know when sea trout 'are up'!

Happily for visiting anglers and tourists, the summer produces the best trout and sea trout fishing. Not everyone relishes early spring or late autumn salmon fishing in ice-cold rivers and in wild weather. In summer, fishing for trout in rivers and lochs is comfortable and fascinating. And on summer nights, angling for sea trout can be a thrilling experience.

There is no closed season for coarse fishing and the anglers who fish for roach, pike or bream in Scottish waters are in their element on river banks in any kind of weather and in all seasons.

Alternatives with a rod and line

River trout are coming into their own in Scotland as never before. This is an impression I get increasingly from anglers who complain about the alternatives for their sport with rod and line.

Of course, good salmon fishing was never an activity for people with a small pocket. Certainly association and club waters could offer daily or weekly tickets at reasonable prices; the Spey, the Tay, the Aberdeenshire Don and other rivers like the Nith and the Annan all have local associations who behave very decently to visitors and make moderate charges. But, let's face it, getting on to really good salmon beats on the Tweed, the Aberdeenshire Dee, or on to the highly-valued parts of the Spey and the Tay, has always been prohibitive for all but the better-off fishers. And, in a way, that is

probably as it should be. Riparian owners have to make an income from their rented waters that will pay their keepers and ghillies (and their taxes) on the intake from a few anglers in quite a short season.

The problem is now becoming worse for the ordinary British salmon angler — even for one with a large enough pocket. Exclusive beats on the Tweed are being rented at exhorbitantly high rates. The pressure from foreign tourist-anglers from America, Europe and now from Japan, for good fishing stretches makes it difficult for river owners to resist the dollars, the marks and the yen. The result is higher and higher rents for the best river beats. The market dictates the rate and the trend is supply and demand.

Another alternative for keen sports fishermen

The author on the Earn.

28

(and women) is loch fishing, mainly for trout. This activity, too, is increasing as is the demand for boats on the better waters. Loch Leven usually has a waiting list in summer and the Lake of Monteith is also fairly well booked in advance; weekends are almost impossible for a visitor in summer. Of course, there are plenty of other less well known lochs and reservoirs that have good fishing waters. Those nearest to the populated centres of Glasgow, Edinburgh and Dundee are heavily booked. Those farther north, towards the Highlands, are very varied in their facilities for visiting anglers. Some have boats, some do not and some, in my experience, might be safer without the boats they offer!

Other lochs in the far north, in Caithness and Sutherland for example, are an angler's paradise. Beware, like most Shangri-las, they take some effort to reach. And there is no hard-and-fast rule that says the more remote a loch is, the better will be the fishing. Indeed, in my experience of trekking over peat-moors and up small mountains in the Highlands, far away hill lochs produce no heavier than ½ lb trout, or less, because in their acidic waters fish feed poorly and growth is restricted.

There are exceptions — the lochs around Kinbrace in Sutherland (Loch Rimsdale and others) produce trout of a respectable size and I have seen three-pounders come out. But the point I make is that an angler in such areas must be physically fit!

A few years ago some game fishers I knew, on seeing the rising prices and other factors affecting their sport, turned to sea angling. Certainly they were following an increasing number of people of all ages all over Britain who took up this side of the sport. Adherents of sea angling will tell you of some obvious advantages – fishing in the largest water in Europe that contains millions of fish, namely the sea; the availability around our coasts of boats for charter; the sea angling clubs that offer cheerful company and the fact that there is always safety in numbers. And the best advantage of all — the certainty of bringing home something, even if only a few mackerel.

Strangely, these enthusiasts are not quite so vocal today, at least in Scotland. For one reason or another (it depends on who is giving you the reason) catches of fish by sea anglers in the Clyde estuary have been dropping dismally over the past few years. Boat skippers have told me it is the fault of commercial fishermen, who now trawl their nets inshore right through the traditional angler's areas. Be that as it may, there is no doubt that the number of anglers fishing one-time excellent grounds off Gourock, or around Whiting Bay in Arran, or up the sea lochs around the Kyles of Bute, are now fast decreasing. The same story concerns sea angling in other parts of the Scottish coastline. Those brave souls who do not go out to sea in chartered boats with a group but sail out in pairs in small craft, frankly take their lives in their hands and are often the main worry of the coastguards. There are tragedies almost every month from spring to autumn.

Coarse fishing? The unspeakable fishing for the uneatable, as Oscar Wilde might have put it? Well, there are seven clubs now and a Scottish Federation for Coarse Angling, but for all the element stimulating competition in this sport, I have yet to meet an enthusiastic game fisher who has 'changed sides'!

Where does this leave the game fisher who says, 'It's the fishing — not the fish'? Where does he go; the ordinary angler who is not necessarily a cheery chappy desperate to be out with the boys? The angler who wants peace, the music of birdsong and a gentle breeze that ripples the water of a trout pool? The fisherman who likes the chessboard pattern of sunlight through the trees as he contemplates a gently-running stream and hears the babbling of a chattering river on a summer afternoon? Or the angler who wades silently in the deep rose-coloured dusk to cast his flies on the mirror-smooth water of sea trout haunts and has his battle at sunset with a fighting dervish on the end of his line?

I make no pretence of being anything else but biased in favour of rivers and of trout and sea trout. If I were not, I could put forward the more popular viewpoint that loch fishing is more productive, requires less effort and creates more stimulating competition. I could also point to those excellent association salmon waters that will welcome a visitor for a few pounds a day. Or, I could take you out on the North Sea with the Big Cod fishers who bring back twenty-pounders galore.

I could do all of these things. But, living and fishing in Scotland has been enriched for me by one kind of angling above all others — the rivers and their trout.

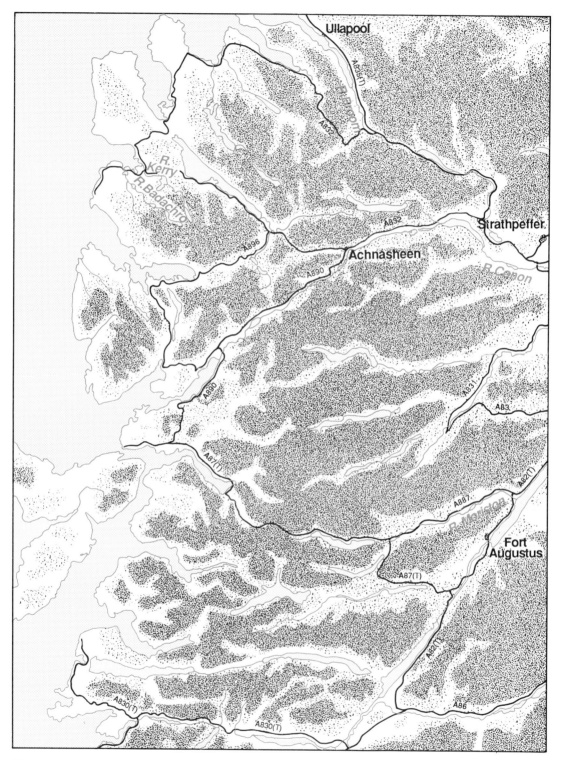

The Far North

The rivers

Naver · **Inver** · **Berriedale** · **Wick** · **Alness** · **Wester** · **Badachior** ·
Kerry · **Broom** · **Polly** · **Grimersta**

A good day's catch.

Never, Never Naver

After a recent newspaper item reported the sale of the fishing rights on the River Naver in Sutherland for £2 million, I enjoy seeing the staring eyes and open mouths of angling friends when I casually say, 'I had a few days on the Naver this season.'

'You're joking!'

'Cross my heart.'

Then I wait in silence while they run it through the money machine in their minds. Over £1,000 for a week's fishing! 'Let's see, now — per day that would be . . .'

What I do not tell them (unless they ask) is that I paid only a few pounds each day for my three days on this famous, fabulously expensive, river in Sutherland, normally fished by the very well-heeled, usually foreign guests at the hotel in Altnaharra.

Yes, it is true that fishing the Naver for salmon, on any beat from Loch Naver down the twenty miles, can cost an angler over

The Naver estuary at Bettyhill where sea trout come in with the tide.

£1,000 for a week's glorious fly fishing in a scenic paradise. And for me that would probably mean never-never land. What is not true is that the river is closed to an avid trout or sea trout angler with a light purse.

I fished from a point above the Bettyhill Bridge to the mouth, a distance of about two miles. This is 'local' water and it must be said that only a certain number of visitors' tickets are allowed on any one day. It is sensible to make a personal reservation in advance, preferably with an introduction from one of the hotels. Sea trout fishing here is very good and large brown trout up to 3 lb are frequently taken. My bag on each day was not spectacular, a sea trout and four brown trout, but the fishing, the surroundings and the near-misses combined to make it a memorable trip.

It is a matter of opinion whether the Thurso, the Helmsdale, or the Naver is reckoned to be the best salmon river in northern Scotland. In one way, the Naver has the best of nature's deal for a first-class river for migrating fish, for salmon and sea trout. It flows from Loch Naver, which is six miles long and which in turn is fed via Loch Meadie by the River Mudale. Along its course, the Naver is fed by the Mallart river before it runs through some of the most beautiful forest and moorland scenery in Scotland to reach Torrisdale Bay, a panoramic estuary out from Bettyhill.

While on the subject of salmon, an interesting custom is exercised each season by the Naver Fishery Board, who present a salmon to every old age pensioner in Bettyhill and to every house in Strathnaver. In addition, any ratepayer in Bettyhill may purchase a salmon for £1.

When on the river, I met a holiday angler, a short, grey-haired, pleasant man from Falkirk, who said he had been coming to this part of Sutherland for twenty years. He stayed in a furnished cottage near the river for two weeks and fished every day on this few-pounds-a-day stretch near the estuary.

While I shared a cup of coffee from his flask, he said, 'What flies are you using?'

'Two flies — a Teal and Blue on the tail and a Greenwell's Spider on the dropper.'

'You're not a salmon man, then?'

'I've never refused an offer from a salmon on the water. Are you telling me that salmon might have a go for my tail fly on this part of the river?'

'It's been known,' he said. 'But why don't you hedge your bets and put a wee Stoat's Tail on your cast?'

'How wee?'

'Oh — say about size twelve.'

'For a *salmon*?'

'Yes — a tube fly.'

'Show me,' I said, producing my fly box to let him select what he was talking about.

'You don't have one,' he said. 'I have a few.' He produced a small dark-blue-and-grey Stoat's Tail tube fly and a tiny treble hook.

'And that's it?' I asked. 'For salmon?'

'Or sea trout. Or a brown trout around here. You'll get the occasional estuary trout going for a fly like that.'

'You amaze me. I can understand a sea trout being attracted to it — but salmon — ?'

'Take my word for it. It's what the locals use on this part of the river.'

Thus armed and ready for anything, I waded into the water and began casting towards the trees on the far bank. It would delight me to say how instantly effective was my friend's Stoat Tail and to give a blow-by-blow account of my conflict with a salmon. The fact is that I attracted no fish resident or migratory for three hours. Then, at long last, a sea trout took the fly, the rod bent over, the reel screamed and I had him on. When netted, the fish was just over 2 lb and that was the pinnacle of my day.

I met my friend from Falkirk again on the river bank and we had out final coffee before a few last casts. He had no fish but admired my humble sea trout.

I said, 'I wonder why everyone up here fishes in the *lochs* for trout.'

'Simple. That's where they are.'

'But they're in the rivers, too.'

'Who's interested in trout on a salmon river – specially if you've paid a fortune to fish it? Let's face it, up here in the north, you fish for salmon in the rivers and trout in the lochs and rarely the twain meet. Salmon's the King here.'

'Even although the river's full of trout and sea trout?'

'Correct.'

After we parted, I had another look at my 2 lb sea trout, and was well content. There was nothing never-never about that.

Roadside Rivers (Inver)

One way or another, roadside rivers are a menace. For riparian owners they are almost impossible to guard against poachers night and day. For motorists who happen to be keen anglers they can cause accidents, when the driver, as I have often done, cranes his neck and jumps up and down in the car to see if the water is in good trim. Campers are often dubbed as poachers. Even ordinary families having a picnic can have problems explaining to a gamekeeper why little Harry is casting a worm on a hook into the water.

The last time I almost got myself into trouble on a river that ran beside a road was just a short time before the Royal Wedding. I will not name the river in case others may be tempted to cast a rod in those forbidden waters.

I had never fished this river before and when I bought my £2 ticket for the association water, I had only a vague idea how to get to the river and — what was more important — what stretch of it I was allowed to fish. Oh, yes, there was a map on the back of the ticket, but it's a different matter when you're in your car and tearing up a wee Highland road looking for signs that correspond with those on the map.

It was a marvellous-looking river — beautiful, sun-glistening, blue, water snaking all the way down from the mountains. And not another angler in sight.

So I set up my rod and went down through the trees and over the moor to that magnificent torrent which I felt certain was so stiff with fish I could walk across it on their backs. And I had a great time for about an hour, even though I caught no fish.

I never even saw the man coming up behind me, and I certainly couldn't hear him above the roar of the water. Then I heard his voice in my ear, 'Good morning.'

'Morning.' I reeled in my line.

'Are you enjoying yourself?'.

I smiled. 'Great. This looks a really marvellous river.'

He was tall, broad-shouldered and tweedy. 'I think you're a bit out of your way, aren't you?'

I stared at him. 'Am I?'

Then I remembered my £2 association ticket and I took it out of my pocket to show him.

'Oh, but that's all right. I have a ticket. I got it at the tackle shop.'

He didn't even look at it. 'Come on up the road. I have my shooting brake and if you follow me down-river I'll show you where the association stretch is.'

'Whose stretch is this, then?'

He just smiled. 'Well, let's just say it's pretty private and it's pretty expensive *and* I wouldn't like to think you'd caught all the fish and left none for the important visitors next week.'

He didn't even tell me who the visitors were — and I didn't ask. He was very nice about it and led the way for miles down that road till we got to my £2 stretch, then wished me luck.

'After all', he said, 'the *fish* don't know the difference, do they?'

'No,' I said. 'They don't. Who are the visitors you're expecting?'

And he told me.

There is one river on the west coast of Scotland in the far north which reminds me of this experience — the Inver, from which, of course, comes the name of the nearby fishing village of Lochinver. The reason is that for most of its length the river runs alongside the

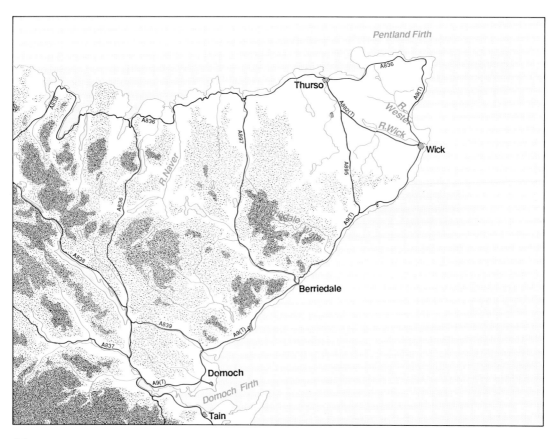

main road, and I often feel that the owners of the fishing must have a difficult task preserving the rights.

It would be foolish to pretend that sea trout fishing on the Inver is supreme. The fish disease Ulcerative Dermal Necrosis (UDN) was first noticed in the river in 1971, and although this disease is noted for its effect on salmon, the sea trout have declined since then due, it is felt, in some measure, to UDN.

The Inver is predominantly a salmon river, yielding about 300 fish a year to rod and line. As far as brown trout fishing is concerned, it should be remembered that in this part of the north-west, the good trouting is largely confined to the scores of excellent lochs in the hills.

The Inver is a spate river, but its wild moods have been moderated because it flows on its five-mile course from Loch Assynt, which is a superb trout fishery managed and controlled by Inchnadamph Hotel. Anglers on the loch frequently hook a salmon or a sea trout. About sixty salmon and scores of sea trout are taken on the loch every year.

No great beauty (Wick)

Salmon anglers who fish the glorious sun-dappled beats on the Tweed, or under the ice-blue sky of a spring Speyside, can say all they care about fishing in a beautiful environment; their main objective is the fish and not necessarily the fishing. In my opinion, this is the main difference between the salmon and trout angler. Of course, both hunt their quarry. Of course, both develop their expertise to an art form. And only a fool would suggest that either kind of angler is a 'meat hunter'.

But what is at the foot of the difference, particularly these days, is money. The salmon fisher who has just paid hundreds of pounds to fish a beat on a good river does not have much time or inclination for bird-watching or observation of river-side life. The rent he has paid concentrates the mind wonderfully — on salmon. This is one of the reasons why, on the rivers which have salmon, sea trout and brown trout in them, only the King of Fish gets all the attention.

Only the trout angler, particularly the brown trout angler, has the time and the patience and the energy to look around, listen, savour the atmosphere of the river and even sit down on the bank to await the rise for flies. Perhaps this is why a trout angler is the first to be switched on or off by the look and the 'feel' of a water before he even unfastens the flies from the rod. And he is the first to wonder why on earth he is here at all if the river is unattractive and devoid of natural beauty.

These thoughts sprang to mind the first time I came across the Wick river in Caithness. A friend and I had been fishing Loch Watten — that is the big loch along the north coast of Scotland from Thurso. We had had our fill of those magnificent brown trout from the loch, fishing most days and many nights (it is quite light up there at 2 a.m.). We went into Wick and found the river. We walked along the bank upstream for a mile or two and I formed the opinion that that river would not register anywhere near the top of my popularity poll for good looks.

The Wick rises from three streams to the south of Watten village. Then it is joined by the water coming out of Loch Watten and flows nine miles or so to the sea at the town of Wick. The part of the river we saw was canal-like and fringed by unpassable, tall weeds until there were a few breaks of faster-flowing runs which looked very fishable.

Down in the lower reaches of the river, they tell me, sea trout fishing is very good; and I do not doubt this.

For all the unattractive appearance of the river, the Wick Angling Association is very active with about 300 members of all ages, and they sell permits to about 150 visitors every year. Of course, salmon is the main interest and the Association concentrate on the hatchery they run. They stock the river with 150,000 salmon fry every year. The Highland River Purification Board have also been very active on the river and their anti-pollution measures have been very effective.

In my opinion, such a well-organised angling association deserves to manage a better-looking water than the Wick I saw on that June day.

Fishing on the edge of the world (Berriedale)

Travel up the A9 along that very open, exposed, coastline from Dornoch and you are now skirting the North Sea. Beyond the harbour of Helmsdale there is hardly any shelter or haven till you reach Wick. This is the wild, naked, north-north-eastern edge of Scotland

riverside beauty. They are the Berriedale, Langwell and Dunbeath waters.

The Berriedale flows through a surprisingly beautiful little glen in one of Caithness's really hilly areas. It is about twenty miles long but only twelve miles of it are fishable, although there are forty-one named salmon pools. The salmon come out about seven or eight pounds and sea trout fishing takes place in July and August. The river also has some good brown trout fishing.

You can get a good view of the river from North Brae, just above the village of Berriedale.

A typical Highland cascade.

where the very names of the villages have the sea-smell of icy winds in them — Latheronwheel, Lybster, Ulbster, Sarclet and Thrumster. Then beyond Wick there is Stayigoe, Noss Head and Nybster just below John O'Groats.

This is the eastern land of Caithness, a county noted for its excellent trout lochs. On this windswept coast line are three small rivers worth the attention of an angler who hungers for the privacy of wildness and rare scenic

The middle beat of the river is the most popular one and it is approached from the croft of Upper Borgue. The river was made available to the public in the sixties and it is stocked every year with 5,000 sea trout fry as well, of course, as salmon fry. There must be some big brown trout in the water because a Mr A. Sutherland caught a 6½ lb and a 3 lb brown trout in the pool above the falls. So far as big salmon are concerned, at Longwell House there is a cast of a salmon weighing 62 lb taken in the nets at the mouth of the river in 1905.

The Langwell river is smaller than the Berriedale but, of course, in these northern spate rivers, size means little when a trickling burn can become a roaring, peat-coloured torrent in a matter of hours. It is a very dangerous river to fish at the part where there is a narrow gorge. There are four respectable salmon pools and some habitats for sea trout.

To the north of both these rivers is another small spate water, the Dunbeath. The source of this river is in the hills at a place with the almost unpronounceable name of Gobernuis-geach. The Dunbeath is fed by hill streams and by the waters from Lochs Dubh and Raffin and flows through the village of Dunbeath to the sea.

Fishing is not easily available to visitors but an approach to the estate might produce a permit if you look like a genuine angler who fishes in a sporting way.

There are the three kinds of game fish in the Dunbeath — salmon, sea trout and brown trout.

An angler fishing these spate rivers in this part of Scotland, if he is lucky enough to obtain permits in advance, can be sure of one thing — there are no crowded waters, and he is fishing on what seems to be the edge of the world!

The swiftest little river in Scotland (Alness)

The first time I had really heard of the Alness as a sea trout river was when I was on a lecture tour around the Highlands for the University of Aberdeen. I talked and showed slides about angling in Scotland and although it seemed to me that this was a bit like carrying coals to Newcastle, as it turned out the tour was a great success. I was amazed at the scores of members of local angling clubs around the Highlands who came to hear about trout and salmon fishing in other parts of Scotland. I realised then how localised is much of Scotland's angling and how strongly the local anglers feel about 'their' particular water.

The Naver estuary in the far north.

It so happened that one of my dates on this tour was in the village hall at Alness. There was a good turnout of anglers with their wives and friends, and during the discussion after my talk I heard from these local fishers about the Alness. I was more interested in their pride in their little river — it is only about twenty miles long from source to mouth — than, I am sure, they were interested in my talk. They really loved the river and the members of the Alness Angling Club invited me to fish it as their guest at any time.

Back in 1909, the angling author, W. L. Calderwood, suggested that the river was considered (it probably still is) the swiftest in Scotland. Certainly it does not have far to travel from its source, at Loch Morie in the mountains of Kildermorie deer forest, down in a north-easterly route to empty into the Cromarty Firth. Salmon ascend the river against very rough torrents when there is a spate, but sea trout fishing is the main attraction for local anglers. About 200 sea trout are caught each season.

The tidal stretch of the river has two main pools, Bridge Pool and the one below it. There are other runs and shallow pools which are covered by the incoming tide and these are well worth a few casts for finnock and sea trout. The finnock fishing peaks in April. This estuary stretch will only fish well, however, when there is a good run of fresh water from the river.

Sea trout are the best angling quarry here, because the salmon usually run straight through to their spawning areas upstream. As usual in such sea trout waters, evening and night fishing in July and August can be very rewarding. Worm fishing is allowed but sea water kills off worms very quickly and the most stimulating and rewarding angling method is with a two-fly cast.

The wee Wester in the far north (Wester)

Away up in the north-east corner of Scotland, only a few miles south of John O'Groats, is a little, unsung, river running out of a small loch. Both are so insignificant that some angling guides do not bother to mention them. The river, if it can aspire to be called that, is called by some the Burn of Lyth and by others by its proper name, the Wester, because it rises in Loch Wester.

The loch lies in a wild, remote, moorland area called Wester Ross and the river runs from it down through Keiss Links and the pleasant sand dunes at the beach to the sea at Sinclair's Bay. This is the only large bay on this coastline and it lies between Noss Head and Tang Head on an otherwise unprotected, naked edge of Scotland facing the North Sea.

The river is only a few miles north of Wick and can be reached by the main A9 road which takes a right-hand fork at Reiss.

It is only about a mile long and fifteen to twenty-five yards wide and quite shallow. Yet it is a delightful little water to fish for sea trout. There is also brown trout in the water and salmon weighing up to 10 lb ascend it to spawn in the loch in the autumn.

That this tiny river, so far north in Caithness, is good for sea trout fishing is unusual, since few far north rivers — even the famous Thurso — have a reputation for sea trout. This area is mainly salmon and loch trout country.

Most anglers fish the river with a short trout rod of nine feet and although I recommend this — be warned! Salmon do not know whether the fly being offered is on a long or a short rod.

Two small rivers in Wester Ross (Badachro and Kerry)

Some fishing guidebooks will tell you that the little Badachro river has no run of sea trout and others will say the reverse. Whatever the truth, it is one of those many spectacular, turbulent, small, rivers in Wester Ross which support salmon but which is not noted for runs of sea trout.

What is very fishable on the Badachro is the slow-moving water in the upper river before the loch empties into it. Brown trout angling with dry fly is very good here in early summer months. When there is a good strong wind with plenty of concealing ripples on the surface of the water, the trout will rise freely.

There is a sister river in this part of the Gairloch that is called the Kerry. It is also a small river but has the advantage of the North of Scotland Hydroelectricity Board at Loch Na H-Oidhche. The loch has been dammed and some of the water diverted to the farm station in the gorge farther down the river. This helps the river with compensation water but does little or nothing for sea trout fishing since few of this fish come into the Kerry.

The Badachro and the Kerry are set in an area of Wester Ross that is particularly wild and beautiful. Their course from the hills represents the best of Scotland's wilderness beauty in the western Highlands.

Beautiful Broom

If you travel by car from Dingwall to Ullapool, any good day in spring or summer, a part of the A835 road offers a view which is breathtaking. At the Braemore junction, take the Ullapool fork and then stop the car and look back towards Strathmore Forest through which flows the River Broom as it runs to the narrow and beautiful Loch Broom. The vista here, seen from above, is one of the finest in the western Highlands and it spans the snaking water of the small river in the valley.

The River Broom has two parts for the keen sea trout angler. From the top of Glebe Pool to the sea there is a tidal stretch which produces good sea trout. When there is a big water on the river, the fish are easier to catch because they come right into the main course of the

Searching for signs of a fish on a Highland stream.

river. The best pool is the Glebe itself which is long and has a retaining bank on the left-hand side.

Many years ago the catches of sea trout were high, both in quantity and size. Fish weighing 12 lb were not uncommon. Today, however, the sizes have waned considerably and the upper limit is around 7 lb. Finnock are there too, of course, and these small virgin sea trout give good sport on fly.

The other part of the Broom is upstream, from the top of the river to the tidal pool. Salmon is the main quarry here and the Inverbroom Estate handles the fishing rights.

For sea trout enthusiasts I recommend the lower tidal stretch and advise anglers to pray for a good spate.

Chalkstream tactics for West Highland sea trout (Polly)

Anglers who wear knee-pads and who crouch behind any available cover on a river bank to fish upstream, stealthily with one single fly, will love the Polly. Other big river anglers who are more used to casting big flies into roaring white water will just want to go home. The sea trout on this short, tricky, river in Wester Ross do not take kindly to highly visible, noisy, splashy, fishers and those who fish this way will catch little.

This is probably one reason why the dry-fly experts from the chalk streams of the Kennet and the Itchen in the south do well here, even when two wet flies are used on the cast. In a way this is surprising for a west coast river in the Scottish Highlands — particularly one so far north above Ullapool.

The Polly is quite a small river, being only a few miles long. The whole area around its course is virtually festooned with the fishing waters of the lochs and streams inland from Erard Bay. Loch Oscaig, to the south, is only one excellent sea trout loch. This Estate is a joy to drive in, or just to see, with its towering mountains and sparkling waters.

From the bridge on the Achiltibuie to Lochhinver road down to the sea, the Polly river flows through boggy peat country. This is why it is so deep, slow and sluggish, and the best fishing conditions are when there is a stiff breeze to create waves and ripples on the surface of the water. Then the southern dry-fly angler gets the best advantage with sea trout. Some of these fish, until July, may be as big as 9 or 10 lb.

Apart from those loch-like flats, the river has two good sea pools just upstream from the beach that fish well on summer evenings.

The most unattainable angling river in europe?

Really, any piece of writing about the Grimersta has no relevance for ordinary anglers. It is as far away as Norway and a permit to fish is almost impossible to obtain. Until recently it was a veritable Somme of a battlefield between the people who own it and the people who poach it.

Yet it would be a crying shame not to attempt to describe what some experts say is the finest salmon and sea trout water in Europe.

First — where it is. The river (if it can be described so boldly) is fifteen miles from Stornaway on the Island of Lewis in the Outer Hebrides, off the north-west coast of Scotland. The river, which really begins in a chain of lochs, flows into one of the Roag sea lochs on the west side of the island. Across the Atlantic by a short distance is the island of Great Bernera. The river has always had natural pools but the owners over the years have made certain damming and sluicing alterations, making them better for holding fish and for angling.

Rising in Loch Langavat (which means the 'long loch') the Grimersta is just over a mile long and would be ideal for salmon and sea trout fishing even though the fish fairly bolt through it in their eagerness to reach the lochs. There are four of these lochs, the waters of which are kept alive and active by the constant flow of fresh water from the river. The head water is Loch Langavat, where all the fish go to reach their spawning redds in the hill burns.

Before considering the great population of brown trout in Langavat, or the tremendous sea trout in the whole chain of river and loch, a quick glance at salmon angling is enough to make anyone's hair stand on end. On 28 August 1888 there is a record of one man, Mr Naylor, with one rod catching on fly fifty-four salmon in one day. Today a dozen salmon in a day is quite common. And the record bag for any one season was in 1925 when the anglers caught 2,276 salmon, 591 sea trout and 271 brown trout. In August alone of that year the total catch was 721 salmon. The best bag for a lady was twenty-four salmon caught in one day.

So much for the King of Fish for which, let's face it, most of the privileged anglers go. Fishing for sea trout can well be imagined and the brown trout fishing in the chain of lochs is also excellent; few come out weighing less than a pound. The lochs are shallow and for the most part have a gravelish bottom. This makes for free-rising fish to the fly.

Getting permission to fish this excellent river with its chain of four lochs is, for the ordinary angler with a moderate purse, almost impossible. The owners have rented the fishing waters to a syndicate of about twenty anglers who are allowed to invite friends by arrangement. The whole thing is very well organised and there is a comfortable lodge. The fishery has a manager, of course, and there is an assistant and twenty-five other staff, including house staff.

I would be scared to ask how much each member of the syndicate pays for a season's fishing.

This very private river and its four lochs were a battleground of controversy some years ago, climaxing in physical violence between the estate ghillies and local poachers who seemed to regard the fishings as part of their traditional privilege. During the season, ghillies are assisted in their duties by students employed by the estate.

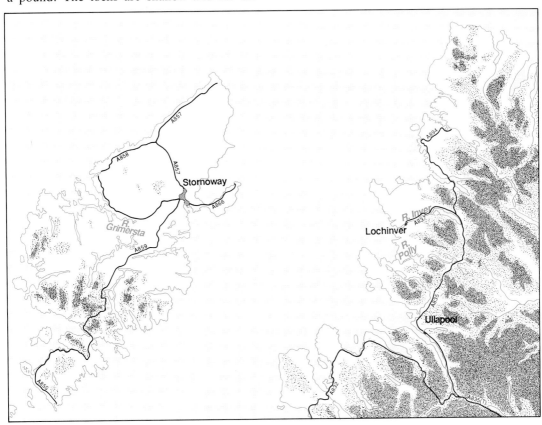

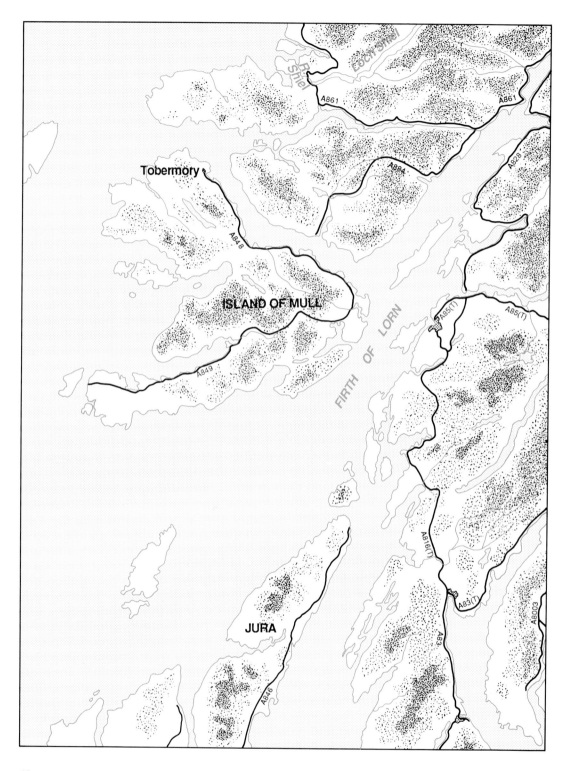

The Highlands

The rivers

Awe · Add · Blackwater · Ness · Moriston · Conon · Shiel

A stream from the Highland moors.

Big fish from a wee river (Awe)

It was a man called W. Muir who saved the day for the River Awe and its reputation for large trout. If he had not caught that record brown trout of 39½ lb in 1866, it is likely that the Awe would have been totally ignored as anything else than one of Scotland's premier salmon rivers. Incidentally Mr Muir's record for a brown trout, caught by rod and line, has not been beaten.

It was inevitable that a fish of this weight — enough to make eyes pop if it had been a salmon — would create controversy. There are now several stories about how the fish was caught. That very reliable bible of the angling scene, *Where to Fish*, stated that the trout was caught in *Loch* Awe, that it was foul-hooked on a trout fly, that it took two-and-a-half hours to land, and that it was set up in a case which was later destroyed by fire.

Then along came Mr Angus McCall (himself no mean angler, he caught a salmon of 53 lb in 1913), who gave a different version of the story. He said that the fish was definitely caught in the *River* Awe in the top pool and not in the loch. This pool, once called McEwan's Pool, is now naturally called the Disputed Pool. He said further that the local people had never been in any doubt on the point. His version of the catch was confirmed by Mr J. Watson Lyall who wrote in his book, *The Sportsman's and Tourist's Guide to the Rivers, Lochs and Deer Forests in Scotland* the following:

'The largest specimen of *salmo-ferox* known to have been taken in Loch Awe or the River Awe was caught in 1866 in the upper pool of the River Awe on a medium-sized salmon fly, by the late Mr Muir of Instryinch, the weight being 39½ lb.'

The controversy did not end here. A well-known authority and author of works on the sea trout said the fish was not a trout at all, that it was more likely to be a stale salmon. But this could never be established as the set-up fish in its case was destroyed by fire, and there were no scales available for identification.

Back to Angus McCall and the local people who said the fish quite definitely was a trout! To support their opinion is the view of two anglers who spoke to Jock Scott, author of the book *Game Fish Records*. They said they saw the fish immediately after it was killed and it was without doubt a brown trout and was caught on a salmon fly in the Disputed Pool.

Whatever the truth of Mr Muir's monster trout and exactly where it was caught, there is little argument in the fact that the Awe is a river of really big fish, although salmon are the main claim for its reputation. Even if Mr Muir's fish proved to be a false claim, another brown trout of 17 lb was caught in the River Awe in 1925 by J. Craig Wilson, and a sea trout of 21 lb was caught in the same river in 1908 by the Reverend A. M. Opcher.

Strangely for a water with such a reputation for big fish, the Awe is a short river — only five miles long. Until the early 1960s it used to start its course from Loch Awe through the Pass of Brander, then roar down three miles to the salt water of Loch Etive. Then the hydro-electric authorities built a 59 foot high concrete barrage across the river which, some say, put an end to catching really big salmon, or trout for that matter. Before the barrage, salmon in the over-50 lb range were caught, including a monster of 57 lb hooked by Major A Huntington in 1921 and, not to be outdone, a fish of 55 lb was caught by his wife six years later. Today, big fish in the 30 lb range are still caught, but it is doubtful if the super-monsters will be seen again in the Awe.

It would be a mistake to class the Awe simply as a river and leave it there. However short it is, the river is the centre-piece in a district of mountains, magnificent scenery and famous fishing rivers such as the Orchy, the Etive, Kinglass, Coe, Euchar, Helland Oude, and the lochs – Awe, Etive, Fyne and Creran. The potential for electric power generation was seen in the thirties and today water in the area is tunnelled, pumped, recycled, barraged and channelled in a complex system that, some say, has done nothing to enhance either trout or salmon fishing. Whether that it is true or not, all the waters in the Awe district are heavily fished by anglers, ranging from trout fishers who go out in boats from hotels around Loch Awe to salmon anglers who pay considerable sums for the beats on the River Awe and other rivers in the autumn.

Inverawe Fisheries at Taynuilt have a mile of the river that is available to anglers. They also have three lochs stocked with brown trout, rainbow trout and, surprisingly, salmon, on which anglers can try their luck. They hire out rods and tackle, give tuition and have father-and-son concession tickets. There are also facilities for refreshments and meals.

The River Awe has never been predominantly a brown trout river for the angler who would just like a few fish in the day and good sport. It is hardly a good sea trout river. But when those fish are caught on this short, five-mile water course, the angler can be sure that what has taken his fly is no minnow.

What kind of river is it, Anyway? (Add)

On a kind of Richter fishing scale ranging from one to ten, a river is good or bad according to an angler's personal experiences and whether it is also a salmon river, or a sea trout river, or a brown trout, pike, grayling, roach or perch river. It took me a long time to realise that the Earn in Perthshire is an excellent grayling river simply because I had never fished for that species in the late autumn when their season starts. And then I thought it an odd coincidence that in some excellent back-end salmon rivers the two kinds of fish are at their most prolific at the same time, albeit in different patterns of water.

Naturally, we consider the upper reaches of the Clyde exclusively as trout water. There are simply no sea trout. Nor are there — now, stop there for a moment. No salmon? Will this be the case in five years' time when, as suggested by the Clyde River Purification Board, they build a fish ladder at Bonnington Linn, upstream from New Lanark, to facilitate the ascent of migrating fish. Then what kind of river will it be? The salmon are already coming through Glasgow in scores as far as Motherwell and are spawning somewhere in this area of the water.

I have yet to read or hear about the Add in Argyllshire as anything but a fine wee salmon river; apart from the fact it always comes first in any index of Scottish rivers. The river is wee — only sixteen miles long — and even back in 1909, when there were far fewer fish-catchers and more and bigger fish generally, W. L. Calderwood wrote that the average weight of salmon caught there was only 7½ lb, though there was record of a very occasional one of over 20 lb.

Many years ago, when I had recently started to learn something about angling, I was invited for a day's fishing on a private stretch of the Add. My host was a retired army colonel who was very expert. There was no question as to how he saw the river. We were fishing for salmon and that was that. How could one think of any other fish on a west coast Highland spate river?

The problem for me, however, was the vast gulf between my host's expertise and my ignorance of the gentle art. I liked the look of the river as soon as I saw it winding elegantly through flat moorland. There were nice, even banks and good casting points at the end of every stream; just at the right spots for putting a fly into the run and letting it drift easily, although controlled, into a deep, dark pool. And for a relative beginner like me who was more used to trout fishing, these things were very important.

Of course, my host had other ideas altogether. As I have said, he was an expert and he talked me out of everything. He talked me out of using my own short rod; then he talked me out of using a Grouse and Claret fly, then out of casting as if for trout, then out of fishing these long, smooth glides. In fact, he nearly talked me out of fishing at all that day.

For most of that afternoon, I really only had one kind of refuge — I kept out of his sight then, about two hundred yards along the river bank, I changed everything. If he had seen me he would have stormed at me. I used my short nine-foot rod and took off the huge Silver Doctor salmon fly he had insisted on and I replaced it with a nice cast of two size 10 trout flies.

As I fished, I occasionally caught sight of him across the moor using his big fourteen-foot greenhart rod and admired his roll-casting technique. I knew he had a big Thunder-and-Lightning salmon fly at the end of his cast but I was as happy as a sandboy working away in the shallower water with my trout flies.

I knew it had to come sooner or later. In the middle of the afternoon he appeared on the bank and he was horrified. 'What on *earth* are you doing? You'll never get any salmon with *that* little rod. Come up here and I'll show you how to use a *real* salmon rod.'

There was nothing else for it. I was caught red-handed. He was my host and he was an expert. So I splashed over to the bank and followed him down to the salmon pool feeling dejected and rebuked.

'Here we are,' he said. 'Have a few casts here.'

I took hold of his big rod. It felt like trying to fish with a flagpole.

'You'll manage, he said. 'Perseverance — that's the secret.'

After a few horrible attempts, even he could see that I was making little of it. He shook his head. 'Well, I suppose if you've only recently started to learn to fish, handling a salmon rod's a bit difficult. Most beginners start on a trout rod.'

'That's what I've been trying to say —.'

'Well, okay, you'll just have to go back to that shallow water and work away as best you can with that little rod of yours.' He sighed.

'Yes, I suppose I will.'

'You won't get anything, y'know.'

'No, I don't suppose I will. But I enjoy it — that's the main thing.'

He smiled indulgently. 'That's right. So long as you enjoy it.'

So I went back to the shallow stretch and cast away happily.

It must have been about twenty minutes later that I felt the 'chug' on my line. So I 'chugged' back and the next thing my rod was bending over like a question-mark and my reel screaming.

I did not see the fish until the end of my fight with him. Even then I imagined it was the biggest trout I had ever seen. My friend heard my shouts and he ran along the bank and netted the fish — a sea trout of 6 lb. It had taken the Grouse-and-Claret of my two-fly cast.

He was open-mouthed. 'Yes, but where were you standing? Over here? In the shallow water? And where did the fish take you? But that's not a sea trout or a salmon pool. People don't catch anything there. And anyway, this is a salmon river.'

I kept apologising and saying how sorry I was to have caught the fish in the right place, with the right fly, at the right time, with the right rod, but that I could not help it.

The experience taught me something. If you are a beginner, the fish don't know who is at the other end of the line, whether it is an expert or an ignoramus. Nor do they care.

In 1955, the North of Scotland Hydro-electricity Board started a scheme which entailed trapping the headwaters of the whole Add catchment above Lechuary Glen and creating diversions so that, today, the river depends on heavy rain because compensation flows are used on the river. Together with other afforestation schemes, this has done little to improve fishing on the Add for either salmon or sea trout.

For all this, it is a wild, beautiful little river embodying the best appearance and terrain of a west Highland spate river. And the sea trout fishing gets better the nearer the estuary you go, even though this means some careful timing of the tides.

Beautiful Blackwater

No one would seriously suggest that salmon fishing in the Conon River district had been ruined. In spite of early criticisms, when the Hydroelectricity Board virtually took over the Conon (the largest river in Ross-shire) salmon fishing is still good in spite of the building of nine dams, miles of pipelines and aquaducts and six power stations. In one way, it is a miracle that migrating fish have continued their spawning runs since these schemes started many years ago.

The River Conon rises in the magnificent and beautiful deer forests of Inchbae, Strathvaich, Strathgarve and others, and is fed by four large tributaries, the Blackwater, the Bran, the Meig and the Orrin. The largest tributary is the Bran, which rises west of Achnasheen.

Looking at a map of the River Conon district is a baffling experience. Water is piped, dammed, purified and channelled in a geographic maze of lochs and rivers, to such an extent that it would totally confuse a visitor looking for a place to fish. The area suffers from an over-abundance of fishing water. But the salmon angler who does not mind paying a goodly sum for his week's fishing, will have little difficulty in finding a good beat, either on the Conon itself or on one of the tributaries. Nor does the trout angler have to look far for sport in this county of hundreds of lochs.

What about the river trouter. Where does he go? It is unusual to find a river in the Highlands of Scotland which is not noted for its salmon but the Hydroelectricity Board has built a reputation for brown trout. Perhaps trout anglers should be grateful to the Board for having created all the power stations, dams, aqueducts and funnels around the rivers between Strathpeffer and Dingwall and farther North.

The Conon has four main tributaries and for the brown trout angler, in my opinion, the greatest of these is Blackwater. (It all depends on the guide book or fishing manual whether the name of the river is written as all one word or two separate words.)

There are three beats on this river. The bottom beat starts at Bridge Pool just below Achilty Bridge and ends at Junction Pool where the river joins the Conon. The river between the salmon pools all have good brown trout in them, some weighing around the 2-lb mark. Dry-fly fishing is used here a lot.

The middle beat starts from Rogie Falls above Achilty Bridge. Back in 1963 this beat was enlarged to a section of the left-hand bank of the Conon. This extra bit is part of Boat Pool.

Now we come to the river trout anglers' happy hunting ground — the top beat. This part of the river extends from the outflow at Loch na Croic to just above the Falls of Rogie. Access to the beat is from the housing estate of Tor View at Contin and from there by the forestry road to Rogie Farm. Trout fishing on this beautiful part of the Blackwater is well worth an effort to get there. Trout of over 4 lb are taken each season and the average fish is well over 1 lb. The beat is managed by the local angling club and permits to fish are most reasonably priced at a few pounds per day.

Angling in the capital of the Highlands (Ness)

There is at least one good thing about fishing a river which runs through a town; you never have to look far to get a permit. Most fishing

The River Lochy.

tackle shops sell tickets and the charges are usually very modest in those towns and cities that adjoin a river.

The Ness, which runs through the capital of the Highlands, Inverness, is no exception. Although the main population of fishers on the river are salmon anglers (they are hard at it from 15 January when the river opens) sea trout and brown trout fishing on this short six-mile river should not be ignored. Inverness Angling Club controls the fishing on three miles of the river, from the south side of the town beyond Holm Mills to the north of the river where it enters the Beauly Firth.

The river is not a water for absolute beginners, whether fishing for trout, sea trout or salmon. The locals know exactly where to go and my advice is to tack along, watch what they do and follow suit, at a reasonable and sportsman-like distance.

May and June are the best months for sea trout which come up in shoals from the Firth. The place to be on an early summer evening is at South Kessock. The fishing starts 400 yards west of Kessock south pier for a distance of about two miles west. Crossing the Firth, fishing is also allowed from 830 yards west of what was the north pier, to a point 600 yards east of Craigton Cottage. You are not allowed to fish from a boat in this area.

The estuary fishing on the Ness for sea trout can be superb. It is not particularly noted for an abundance of sea trout over 2 lb, but never forget that the largest sea trout caught on the river was 9½ lb and the largest brown trout 7½ lb. While writing about the abundance or size of fish on this river it should be mentioned that, in 1876, Mr Denison caught seventeen salmon on the fly in one day.

River of the big trout (Moriston)

If I were a stranger to the Loch Ness area and wanted a day's fishing on the River Moriston, I would feel glad to be a trout angler. Yes, the

salmon are there all right. And anglers fish for them in the loch itself and in the various rivers that empty into the loch. But the whole area appears to have had its waters dammed, aqueducted, pipelined, tunnelled and harnessed for hydroelectric power. A look at any map shows a maze of water abstraction and divergence schemes.

This is not to say that the North of Scotland Hydroelectricity Board have constructed these water-power schemes with no thought to the fishing. On the contrary, this organization has used tremendous amounts of skill and finance in order to preserve the excellent salmon fishing there. But for a stranger to set up his fishing rod on the Moriston without fairly intimate knowledge, might lead him to settle for the river's resident brown trout.

The Conon, Easter Ross.

The lower half of the river, from Torgoyle Bridge downstream to Dundreggan Dam, is managed by Glenmoriston Estates, from whom permits can be arranged. Trout fishing starts on 15 April and goes on till the end of September and this part of the river is famous for its trout. Some local anglers put back fish of 1 lb or less! Many fish in the 3 to 5 lb class are taken.

The trout angler should really take time to explore all the waters and hills around here. The scenery from Invergarry along the Caledonian Canal to Fort Augustus, then on to Invermoriston, is magnificent and trout fishing in the various rivers and hill lochs is plentiful and reasonable in price.

The River Moriston begins its life as part of a water system coming from Loch Cluanie and Loch Loyne and flows twenty-five miles through one of the most beautiful, wooded, valleys in the Highlands, Glen Moriston, to empty into Loch Ness four miles from Invermoriston. The drive from Shiel Bridge under the mountains of the Five Sisters of Kintail down to Loch Ness is quite unforgettable.

Ebb tide on the Conon

The largest river system in Ross and Cromarty is the Conon. It has four tributaries, the Blackwater, the Bran, the Meig and the Orrin and they bring to the main river the peat-stained spates and torrents from the splendours of Highland moors and heathered hills.

So much has been written about and boasted about the salmon of this labyrinthine river system that some people believe that tea made with Conon water would taste of salmon.

Not so often described are the excellent opportunites for sea trout fishing. And the place, in my opinion, where these opportunites are best is at the estuary, from Bridge Pool at Conon Bridge to the tail of New Pool. Like most rivers in this part of Scotland, fishing is by fly only and — particular to this part of the river — thigh waders only. No chest-high waders are allowed. Fishing is from the bank.

In the spring and early summer, much of the angling is for finnock and some baskets of these can be heavy. When the tide is going out and coincides with falling light, the fishing can be tremendous. Small flies are used, invariably 'wee doubles', but a special Conon lure, called the Grey Lure, is effective.

Sea trout fishing is also very good in the bottom beat of the river which extends from Rock Pool above the Cruives at Top Box, down to below Conon Bridge. Here fly and spinning are allowed and an effective lure is a small Mepp spoon.

A wee river and a big loch

When is a river not a river?

One of the most familiar angling geometries in Scotland is a wee short river leading upstream to a long, narrow, loch; so narrow indeed that it is sometimes difficult to say where the river ends and the loch begins. This is the case with the River Awe leading to Loch Awe, the River Echaig leading to Loch Eck and, most famous of all, the short River Leven leading to Loch Lomond. There are many others.

One of these short-legged waters is the River Shiel leading up to Loch Shiel in Argyllshire. The loch is far better known than the river and this is hardly surprising since the river is only three miles long from the point where the loch empties and where the river empties into the sea. The loch is seventeen-and-a-half miles long.

This is a particularly wild and beautiful part of the western Highlands. The loch is enshrouded in history: at the top, north-east end at Glenfinnan there is a monument which commemorates the raising of Bonnie Prince Charlie's standard in 1745. It was here that the ill-fated rebellion army of Highlanders was raised in an attempt to restore the Jacobites to the throne.

For all its short length, the river and its main sea pool must be one of the most frequently

The River Shiel leading to Loch Shiel.

photographed areas in Scotland for the covers of angling magazines. It is highly preserved as a sea trout and salmon water and such sea trout as are caught here are usually large. The main competitors are the occasional seals which boldly come right up to the loch. When the tide is out and the sun has set over the southern arm of Moidart, fishing can be tremendous on the sea loch into which the Shiel flows and the wide slow-moving river as it enters the Sea Pool.

On the loch, dapping and sunk-fly methods account for most of the sea trout catches.

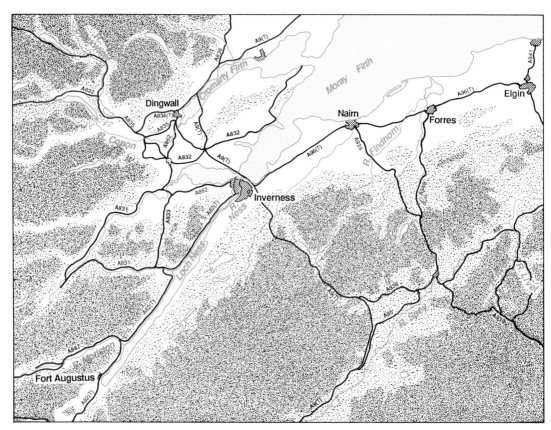

The North East

The rivers

Spey · Don · Deveron · Isla · Bogie · Findhorn · Ugie
Ythan · Livet

The glorious River Spey.

Dry-flying the Don

There was a time, I seem to remember, when the angling press never seemed to be off the Aberdeenshire's Don's back and published long-winded grievances every month. 'The dying Don' and 'What's to be done about the Don?' were typical of their complaining articles. Of course, there was a lot of justification for the grim charges. For years, since the end of the last war, the river *was* badly polluted in the reaches of the lower estuary. Indiscriminate dumping of waste by the paper mills on the outskirts of Aberdeen was the main reason and, of course, anglers complained bitterly over those years.

The complaints are now dying down and there are fewer articles in the fishing press about the issue. Pollution, too, near the mouth of the estuary is also dying down.

Not all anglers complained during those bad years. Let's face it, the people who suffer most from polluted estuaries on rivers are the

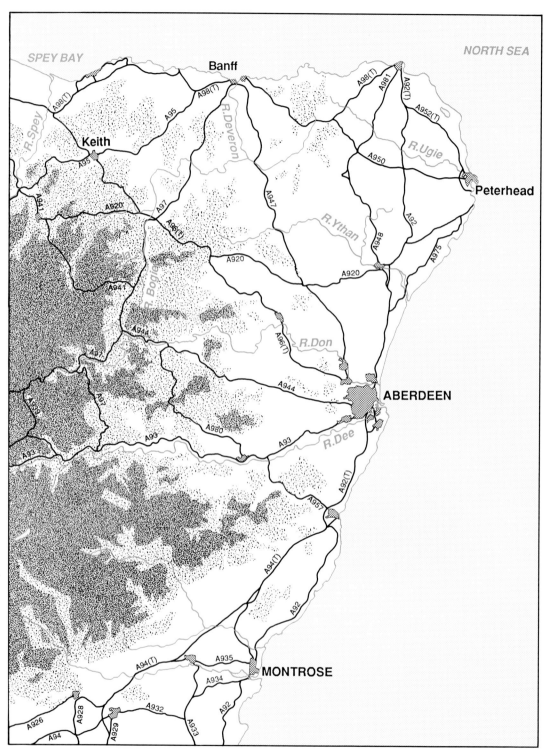

SPEY BAY

Banff

NORTH SEA

R.Spey

Keith

R.Deveron

A98(T)

A95

A98(T)

A981

A98(T)

A92(T)

A952(T)

A95

A941

A920

A97

A96(T)

R.Ugie

Peterhead

A947

A950

A94(T)

R.Bogie

A920

A920

R.Ythan

A948

A92

A975

A944

A97

A96(T)

R.Don

A99

A93

A980

A944

ABERDEEN

A99

A93

R.Dee

A92(T)

A957

A94(T)

A92

A935

MONTROSE

A94(T)

A934

A928

A932

A92

A926

A929

A933

A94

salmon anglers. Migrating fish cannot get through the oxygen-starved waters to get upstream to spawn and so fish stocks decline. That is what was happening on the Don, sister river of the world-famous Royal Dee only a few miles on the other side of Aberdeen. Now, with the situation under better control, the fishing is improving season by season and salmon anglers are getting good sport again.

Mercifully, trout fishing has not been affected. When I think of Don trout, I think about that magnificent stretch managed by the Grant Arms Hotel at Monymusk, or that wonderful water at Alford (pronounce it Afford). I also think about those splendid yellow-belly trout and, to my mind, the Don is the finest brown trout river in Scotland.

There is only one rewarding way to fish for trout on the Don, I think, and that is by dry fly. Not only is it more productive, but bigger trout are caught. The sheer joy of being by oneself in those sylvan reaches around Monymusk, for instance, is something that will live in the memory of an angler for years. 'Reading' the water on the Don is a skill worth improving day by day. On many chalk streams in the southern part of Britain (particularly the famous ones such as the Test, or the Avon, or the Kennet) stalking trout, keeping down out of the skyline behind bushes and carefully aiming the cast so that the single fly alights right on the spot above the rings of a feeding fish is a highly-practised skill, never to be decried. 'Reading' a well-oxygenated water like the Aberdeenshire Don, however, is another matter. I have fished there with experts, like Johnnie Muir, who could actually see where a trout was feeding on the every edge of the white water at a tumbling cascade, but you or I might strain our eyes for ages without seeing the slightest sign of a fish.

The Don starts its life in an area (mentioned in the BBC's weather reports almost every time there is snow) near the Cock Bridge-Tomintoul district of the Lecht road, which is invariably the first road to be closed during a winter snow-up. It flows for eighty miles

The Royal Dee — rich for salmon, poor for trout.

through such a variety of Aberdeenshire scenery that the river and its fishings might well be described as so many different rivers. Only one thing is constant — the quality of its trout fishing. Through the lonely, beautiful and wild Strathdon, down into gentler Glenkindie and Kildrummy, on to the famous stretches of Brux, Auchintool, Castle Forbes, Alford and Monymusk and on, down through Kemnay and Inverurie, where the landscape is verdant and rolling, the river finally reaches Aberdeen, to empty into the North Sea beyond the Bridge of Don. After Inverurie the surroundings resemble that of an English stream and visitors from the south used to quiet chalk streams will find familiar stretches of water here.

I have fished with flies upstream 'dry' and downstream 'wet' on various parts of the Don. On one occasions, while fishing downstream with a team of three wet flies, a small grilse snatched my tail fly — a Bloody Butcher. No, it did not break my cast. It simply got off. And this gave me a hint of what can happen on the Don when fishing for trout with single-hook flies. Salmon and grilse are often there, right in the water where the trout angler is fishing, and it can be a good rule to use double-hooked flies in pools which look as though there might be a salmon lurking. Playing the fish? Well, the rest is up to the skill of the trout angler who will soon find out how long it takes to get a ten-pounder on a five-pound leader and a ten-pound rod if he has the patience, if the nylon holds and if he can beach the fish or 'wrist' it in the shallows. I never even got the chance with my salmon.

I have fished the Don on four excellent stretches – at Glenkindie, Alford, Monymusk and Kemnay. It would be difficult to remember which gave me the greatest pleasure. Probably Monymusk. The Grant Arms Hotel has exclusive rights on ten miles of water for both salmon and trout and the facilities are first class, with good fishing huts and easy access to the water, to suit every age and degree of experience. At Glenkindie, fishing can be obtained from the Glenkindie Arms Hotel at the very reasonable cost of a few pounds for the day. Further upstream at Strathdon, the price for a ticket is the same and can be obtained at the Colquhonnie Hotel. Incidentally, an angler should not be discouraged here at the apparent thinness of the water; some

really big trout have been caught in these upper reaches of the river. The Kemnay stretch is better known for its salmon fishing, particularly early in the season (I have fished it in the snow!), but trout anglers also have good sport there. But I must say that my dry fly days on a ticket purchased from the Forbes Arms Hotel at Bridge of Alford (twenty-five miles from Aberdeen) have been best for me on this wonderful river.

The areas of Kintore and Inverurie are stretches of water I have not fished but my Aberdeen angling friends swear by their quality for trouting.

In Aberdeen itself, the Aberdeen Angling Association has ten miles of the Don available, on a ticket basis, for visitors.

The flies to use on the Don? Greenwell's Glory, of course, then March Brown with a Butcher or a Grouse and Claret — these are my stand-byes in size 12 or 14.

Taking my various experiences on this river into account, the place I would never fail to recommend to trout anglers is Alford.

The unchanging yellow-bellies of Monymusk (Don)

There are many reasons why some riparian owners, angling associations, and even tourist offices hesitate to give visiting anglers up-to-date, reliable, information about the fishing available in their areas. Strangely, it is not so bad regarding lochs. A loch is generally unchanging and the people who have the right to grant fishing permits and hire out boats (usually the same) are constant year after year, possibly reflecting the fact that the loch is the same sheet of water as it was a hundred years ago. Whether fishing is as prolific as it was is a matter of opinion.

Getting ready on a west coast river.

The situation on a river is different. Change is always happening. In the case of fishing rivers, like the Clyde where salmon are now running, or the Forth and its tributaries where the two 'P's — poaching and pollution — are under better control, change is often for the better. Some of today's excellent, smaller, fishing rivers were not worth mentioning a few years ago. The reverse, of course, is also true.

On many Scottish salmon rivers today, one of the great changes is in ownership. Stretches of reputable rivers are being converted to time-share arrangements and others are simply changing ownership, many at fabulous prices. Fishing hotels change hands and with them the waters also find new owners. Estates are sold and with them the rivers. Angling clubs acquire fresh waters. And in some cases nature itself changes the course or character of rivers.

Another river eccentricity for the angler to embrace is its failure to be consistent mile upon mile along its course. On the Clyde, for example, the further downstream you fish from Abington the larger are the fish. And if no fish-ladder is built at Bonnington Linn, the river will be a salmon water from these falls down through Glasgow and a trout water above them.

I know of ten miles of a first-class river which has some of the finest trout fishing in Britain, with its share of good salmon and sea trout fishing. These ten miles are in a river which is eighty miles long and they have had the minimum of change in many years, thank goodness. I refer to the Monymusk Estate stretch of the River Don in Aberdeenshire. The changes that have happened to the Don, in this part in particular, have been for the better. For years the river towards its mouth was badly polluted, but most of this has now ceased and migrating salmon and sea trout are ascending in increasing numbers to their spawning areas upstream. What has not changed is the excellence of the river's residents — the wild brown trout. (Brown may be a misnomer because Don trout are often called Yellowbellies, for obvious reasons.)

For the avid dry-flyer, I can think of no better water in Scotland, not even the Tweed for all its wonderful trouting. Although the Don is a sister river to the Dee, both flowing through Aberdeen city within a mile or so of each other, they are different fishing waters upstream. Whereas the Dee, in most parts, is a fast-flowing river cascading through the wild splendour of Royal Deeside, the Don is a slower-moving water and winds its way much of the time through rich pasture land. These are generalities, of course. Not all of the Dee is a tumbling, salmon-packed paradise. And not all of the Don is an even-tempered water in which the trout feed in comfort. But the ten-mile stretch through Monymusk Estate takes a lot of beating for the river trouter who likes to fish in beautiful surroundings, on water that is accessible, well-managed and which has fairly predictable opportunities for catching a fair number of good, wild trout.

Like most Scottish fishing rivers, the various fishings on the Don are divided according to the estates which own them. Right up near the beginning of the river are the Edinglassie

Fishings, then Candacraig, Strathdon and so on, right down through Glenkindie, Kildrummy to Alford. Then there are the Castle Forbes fishings, then the Monymusk fishings with that ten-mile stretch right in the heart of the river which, in my opinion, has no equal.

Some anglers who come year after year to this beautiful area of the river may complain that its trout fishing does not compare with bygone days. Anglers on most Scottish rivers today make the same complaint, sometimes with every justification. It must be said, however, that the Don has had some wonderful red-letter days for its anglers. The late Mr Henry Gordon of Manar had his best day's fishing at Monymusk with a trout rod and trout flies when he caught sixty-three trout weighing 87 lb plus, and, for good measure, three salmon. In all, in one day, he caught 112½ lb of fish. He had no gaff or landing net or tailer, so he had to beach each fish or, in the case of the salmon, get it by the 'wrist' part of the tail to land it. As he had no ghillie with him he went to a nearby farm, borrowed a sack and carried his fish off on his back. His next best day, verified by the records, was 68 lb of trout — all caught on the fly.

Incidentally, the salmon record for this same angler on the Don was seventeen fish in a day. His best season was 492 clean fish, excluding those caught in the autumn. This was in 1876.

It is not so unusual on a Scottish river to have salmon and brown trout in one water. Sea trout, yes. When migrating fish and river residents are both there in abundance it could be considered an all-season bonanza. The record brown trout for the Don was a monster of 11½ lb caught on fly. Currently the largest trout caught on the river weighed 6 lb and the largest sea trout 3½ lb — both in the upper part of the Parkhill beat which, incidentally, is remarkably inexpensive to fish at a few pounds per day, and can be reached quickly and easily from Aberdeen.

The price of the fishing at Monymusk, it must be said, is more in keeping with a more-or-less exclusive, highly reputable stretch at something under £20 per day. It is under the control of the Grant Arms Hotel, in the village, and this part of the river has had its share of respectable fish — a brown trout of 6 lb representing a four-year record for size. Sea trout of 3 lb are fairly common as well as the salmon now coming up in increasing numbers. The river here is divided into eleven beats with a maximum of two rods allowed on each beat — one to fish for salmon and one for trout. Very civilised.

For all the exhilarating days fishing for trout at Strathdon, or Glenkindie, or Kildrummy, or Alford, on balance, I feel it is to Monymusk I would return any day.

The Spey and its trout

As trout anglers might look at it, some world-famous fishing rivers in Scotland are spoiled by their own reputation. The Spey is possibly one of them.

Like the Aberdeenshire Dee, the Tay and the Tweed, any mention of trout in fishing hotels or inns along the ninety-mile course of the river can be met with a polite stare. The dedicated trout fisher might be forgiven for thinking that he was being treated 'differently'. Some fishing tacklists, ghillies, riparian owners, fishing hoteliers and local anglers along Speyside try to pretend that there are no trout in the river or, if there are, they should not be there.

These Speysiders have nothing against trout anglers. On the contrary, the hotels and guesthouses in the area welcome them, as they do other tourists. It is just that everyone seems to be interested in only one kind of fish — the salmon. (Indeed, not only on Speyside but right through the Scottish Highlands a 'fish' usually means one thing — the salmon.) This might be the reason why the angling fraternity along the river rarely talk about trout fishing, except in the upper reaches of the water and at Loch Insch, where some monster trout are occasionally caught. For the rest of the river it is salmon, salmon, salmon. And this is understandable. The King of Fish is at the heart of the famous fishing beats such as Elchies, Tulchan and Castle Grant and is, therefore, a great source of tourist and riparian income for the area.

For anglers who enjoy either salmon or trout fishing, one particular aspect of Speyside is outstanding — it offers boundless opportunities for an angler's family to enjoy their holiday. The area is a vacation paradise and there are attractions for non-anglers of all ages, ranging from spectacular and beautiful walks to the many leisure centres, castles to be visited, antiquities and water sports amenities in the area. It would be difficult to imagine a better holiday district for the families of trout anglers than Speyside.

Fishing for trout is more popular in the middle and upper reaches than towards the bottom part of the river, simply because the famous salmon beats tend to dominate the scene there. The river rises in the wilderness area of Corrieyairack Forest in the small Loch Spey and journeys down to the Moray Firth at Spey Bay where it empties into the North Sea. It passes the holiday towns and villages of Newtonmore, Kingussie, Aviemore, Boat of Garten, Carrbridge to Grantown-on-Spey, then runs through the 'whisky' country to Fochabers and its terminus.

I have fished the Spey for brown trout in different spots — at Newtonmore, just upstream of the town and near the road bridge, both upstream and downstream of Grantown, and in a beautiful area a mile or so downstream of Boat of Garten. On each occasion it was excellent. My fish were all of good size — up to 1 lb, with the occasional one over that weight. I fished both wet fly and dry fly, but the most enjoyable sessions were at dusk on the smooth glides near Grantown where I fished for the brownies as I would for sea trout — quietly and with stealth.

Salmon, sea trout and brown trout on the Spey.

On another occasion I obtained a day ticket permit to fish for finnock — virgin sea trout — on the estuarial parts of the river near Spey Bay. I reached this area by motoring along the flatlands downstream from Fochabers. Finnock fishing here, just a mile or so up from the mouth, is grand sport. I used standard size 12 sea trout flies invariably with a Blue Zulu on the tail. I caught four fish each around 1 lb in weight.

Fishing dry fly on the river near Grantown, I used a small size 14 March Brown with good effect (it was early in the season). Wading, was tricky which is not unusual on trout-fishing stretches of salmon rivers.

Lovers of the winter ski slopes around Aviemore and Newtonmore can get a good indication for themselves why the Spey is a river of fairly constant water flow, especially in the spring. The snow-melts from the Cairngorm mountains run down the tributaries of the Truim, the Dulnain, the Feshie, the Nethy and the Avon (they pronounce it 'Ann').

Like that for the King of Fish, trout fishing on the Spey is particularly well managed. As early as 1982, Badenoch Angling Association was granted a Protection Order (the second in Scotland) covering all the catchment area of the upper part of the river, as far down as Loch Insch, including Loch Laggan and Loch Ericht. This Order makes it compulsory for an angler to have written permission to fish, and these permits can be obtained from tacklists, tourist offices and from the hotels in Aviemore, Newtonmore and Kingussie. The Protection Order was renewed in 1988 for another three years. The access to fishing in this part of the upper Spey is estimated to provide good fishing for salmon and trout for 258 rods per day, without discomfort to anglers. The only part of the Spey to which access is withheld belongs to the Royal Society for the Protection of Birds, and forms part of their Insch Marshes Nature Reserve.

The area surrounding Loch Insch is truly wilderness and is very marshy and peaty. The loch holds large pike and some monster trout. The local hotel at Invereschie keeps a boat on the loch and issues permits.

Below Loch Insch, the river and its tributaries are managed by two associations. The Abernethy Angling Improvement Association controls six miles of water up to Boat of Garten

and the Strathspey Angling Association manages the other stretch of seven miles from Grantown to Broomhill Bridge, and twelve miles of the River Dulnain. Only weekly tickets are available to visitors who are staying temporarily in the area. The price of each permit, however, is very reasonable, since it covers fishing for salmon, sea trout and brown trout. Further downstream, although the main interest is in salmon, trout permits are issued by the hotels in Aberlour, Rothes and Fochabers. For the tributaries Avon, Livet or Fiddoch permits for trout fishing can be obtained at Tomintoul and at Dufftown.

For beginners there are plenty of angling courses available on the Spey, for example, at Nethy Bridge and Grantown. At Aviemore there is the Osprey Fishing School, whose tutors take participants on trips to the Spey, the Feshie and to some of the nearby lochs. All these schools welcome children and have special sessions for them.

No description of the Spey and its fish would be complete without mention of the sea trout. I have already described my own experience when fishing for finnock near the estuary, but farther upriver, and in the tributaries, sea trout weighing over 15 lb have been caught. In summer, the time to fish for these tremendous fighters is at the gloaming and into the darkness. I have had excellent fishing standing stock-still like a heron, midway down a quiet pool, letting my single fly (say a Stoat's Tail) float downstream slowly . . . slowly . . . then have felt the wild explosion. Getting it in? Well, there are two schools of thought — mine and George Lilley's. I say give the fish plenty of time to tire itself out before producing the net because sea trout, unlike salmon, have soft mouths and could tear the hook free if given too much pressure. My old Speyside and Findhorn friend George says, 'Rubbish. Strike him at once — and strike him hard. Then get him in without ceremony. Don't give him an inch!'

Who is right? Well, I have fished with George in the dead of a black night and have seen him strike hard every time. The result? Three sea trout weighing 7, 9 and 11 lb!

For my part, my best sea trout was one of 4½ lb caught in a pool of the Avon one lilac evening in June. And I played it long and carefully.

The Spey's great runner-up

There is an old tradition along the Spey that says the gentry fish for salmon by day and their ghillies and the local people fish for sea trout at night. It has nothing to do with the value or the size of fish. The reason is more practical. The time to catch sea trout on the Spey is when darkness is falling, or at night. And a salmon angler, fishing his beat all day, has little energy left to go out on the river again after dinner with sea trout rod and flies. The water is therefore left to the others.

Like most angling traditions, of course, this one gets blurred along the edges as years pass. What does not blur, however, is the fact that the Spey is an excellent sea trout river. John Ashley Cooper, one of Britain's most highly respected angling writers, has this to say in his book, *The Great Salmon Rivers of Scotland*:

> 'It is not widely known that the Spey is certainly the most prolific sea trout river in Scotland. The net-catch is said to be immense, and certainly runs into many tons; and the rod-catch is also big, though largely unrecorded . . . Large specimens frequently reach double figures and one of 18 lb is on record from the middle Spey.'

While spring fishing for salmon on the Spey has everyone's attention, sea trout are the more obliging fish to suit the visiting holiday angler. In the early part of summer, bigger fish start entering the river but the best time to fish is when their smaller brothers weighing 2 lb or so come in shoals in June and July, just in time to greet summer anglers in the popular tourist areas upriver.

The Spey at Fochabers.

A good area to fish for sea trout is where the Avon tributary empties into the main river at Baldindalloch. The river flow and general pattern of water here is ideal for sea trout angling and fish are in abundance, no doubt waiting for a big water coming down the Avon to attract them. This tributary also fishes well for sea trout in July on the beats from Tomintoul downstream which are managed by the local hotels and are very popular.

That the Spey has developed naturally to become, with the Tweed and the Tay, one of Scotland's finest fishing rivers should not be difficult to understand. Unlike many other Scottish rivers, there are neither natural nor man-made obstacles to impede the ascending runs of migrating fish. From its mouth at Spey Bay, up through Fochabers for mile after mile, there is nothing to hinder the passage of salmon and sea trout (if we choose to exclude commercial nets) through cascades and gentle pools, white roughage and deep holes, right up to Grantown. There are no barriers except in the headwaters of the two tributaries, the Tromie and the Truim.

Add to this the great advantage of a constant flow of water from the snows of the Cairngorms and other mountain ranges as they melt in the spring and summer sunshine, and there you have the pinnacle of an angler's ideal river, whether he fishes for salmon, sea trout, or brown trout. The whole scene is made more spectacular for the summer angler when he looks around the famous Spey Valley and can actually see in the blue distance the snow-capped mountains which are feeding the river.

It is my opinion that if the Spey was missing any of these factors — unimpeded and constant flow of water, a 'clearway' for migrating fish, thousands of sea trout, good conditions for brown trout, and fishing permits to suit all pockets — it would still be a river of very high esteem in any angler's book.

The 'clearway' feature of the river can work adversely. There are times when the normally even-tempered Spey gets into an almost uncontrollable rage and fairly roars its way down in yellow spate. When this happens, changes occur to the river bed and, of course, favourite lies of salmon and sea trout become obliterated, or new ones are created. Fortunately floods causing serious alterations are rare. But when they happen, they bring to mind among Speyside people something in the history of the area which they hope may never be repeated — the great Moray Floods of 1829.

This was the worst catastrophe ever to happen on Speyside, and was probably the worst of its kind in Britain. The floods that came roaring down the river that August night also affected all the other rivers in the north-east of Scotland. Four-and-a-half inches of rain fell in one night and the Spey rose to twenty-five feet until the lower part of the river, right down to estuary, looked like one huge loch. Countless sheep and cattle were drowned. The river changed its course. Every single bridge down the whole length of the river was washed away except one, the single-span bridge at Craigallachie, which still stands there today. Houses and farms were swept away.

Happily, nothing approaching this severity has since been known on Speyside and most of the time the river and its tributaries keep rolling along serenely, giving considerable pleasure to thousands of anglers every year. And for the many who do not fish for the King of Fish, there is a great runner-up, the sea trout.

Sea trout on the Deveron

Every angler has a red-letter day. Although I might have preferred mine to be a celebration of trout caught, or even the weight of one monster, I feel almost apologetic in admitting to five salmon in one day in a piece that is intended to describe sea trout on one of Scotland's friendliest rivers.

It happened at the end of March in 1959, when I took the Mountblairy fishings on the Deveron from the Fyfe Arms Hotel in Banff, an excellent hotel which, unhappily, is no more. So early in that bright, snow-fringed, season there was only one other guest in the hotel, a retired naval commander, white-eyebrowed and very crusty because he had been fishing the beat downstream from mine all week and had caught nothing. He asked if he might share my beat and I agreed. He

The Spey at Broomhill.

turned out to be a good companion on the river, although neither of us caught a fish all that week — until the Friday. And that was the Red Letter Day.

There had been a tremendous downpour of rain all Thursday night. The Commander banged on my bedroom door at 7 a.m. 'Up! Feet on the floor! Been raining all night. I know the signs. We'll get fish today!'

We made our own breakfast and by 8.30 a.m. we were fishing the river which was running down that glorious tea colour, the delight of any salmon angler. That day our arms were sore from taking salmon. He got four and I got five.

There — I've told it. And I must moderate my tone by saying that I have never had a day's fishing quite like that since. Nor have I caught so many salmon in one day.

To get back to the scene of my triumph, the Deveron is a river I particularly love because it is an all-round water with brown trout, sea trout, grilse and salmon there for the taking, with the right skills at the right time. Like the Nith in Dumfries-shire, it is a river that, by good management, has been brought back from a very poor state, caused by pollution and poaching, to one of the best fishing waters in the country.

In 1966 there was a strong attempt by authorities to abstract water from the Cabrach area (that is where the river has its source) to supply Aberdeen County. The protests from everyone concerned, and in particular from the angling community, was so strong that a public inquiry was held. Almost at the last gasp, the abstraction attempt was beaten off. Since then the river and its fishings have been steadily improved and today it has excellent angling opportunities, particularly for sea trout.

The Deveron has no lochs along its course, so for all kinds of fishing, even for brown trout, dry spells and rainfall are very important factors. As a generality, in times of heavy rainfall, the beats up-river fish well; in low water, the stretches nearer the sea do better. There are areas around Huntly, for instance, where clear-water upstream worming is permitted in summer months for both brown trout and sea trout.

It is a prolific river along most of its forty-five miles through Huntly, Turrif, Rothiemay, Aberchirder till it empties into the North Sea at Banff. About 3,000 salmon, 1,500 sea trout and countless brown trout are caught in an average season. Fishing areas available to anglers are numerous and although some are privately held, they may be fished at moderate prices. Some are held by hotels for their guests and some, like those around Huntly, for example, are well managed by angling associations that sell daily and weekly tickets.

Downstream from Huntly the River Isla, itself a splendid water for the dry-fly trouter, joins the Deveron at Rothiemay. It is here that the visiting angler from the south can enjoy the tree-lined, gentle, pastoral, surroundings he loves in his home waters. Brown trout angling from Rothiemay downstream is excellent, with many a rod-bender to catch.

Another memorable experience on the Deveron was with my friend George Lilley, when we were fishing for sea trout at night on a beat a few miles upstream from Banff. Fishing in total darkness was a new experience for me, although I knew George was truly expert. Sea trout fishing at night in June and July is popular on the Deveron and George had fished this way many times before. I did what he did. I put on a single fly, a Stoat's Tail, and allowed it to drift downstream so slowly that it hardly moved at all in the shallow reaches of the pool. Waiting for that thrilling pull, and not knowing where the fly was, needed a lot of patience and a lot of trust in George's method. I managed to hold on to my self-respect with two sea trout, both over 2 lb and I thought quite well of my skill until I got back to the fishing hut where George was weighing his catch — three sea trout weighing 7 lb, 5 lb and 3 lb.

On another part of the Deveron they use quite a different kind of lure when fishing for sea trout. I was neither attracted to it nor did I see anyone making much success with it, but it is surely the most unusual lure ever used in Scotland. It is called the Banff Nail and they fish with it using a spinning rod on the tidal stretch of the river between Banff and the sea. The lure is nothing more than a three-inch nail through which a hole is bored and a treble hook fixed at the end of it. They told me that sea trout mistake it for a sand eel.

Although the Deveron is a something-for-everyone kind of river, it is the excellence of its sea trout fishing that brings out so many local and visiting anglers on summer evenings to fish quietly and with stealth at the end of even-flowing pools. Size 10 flies are popular for sea trout and the patterns of Blue Zulu, Teal and Silver and Grouse and Claret are recommended.

Where to stay if you wish to fish the Deveron? There are no problems. Huntly, Turrif, Rothiemay, Banff or MacDuff are excellent centres for holidays and amenities. For all the beauty of the surrounding countryside and coastline, the Deveron area is not on the more popular touring routes like Speyside or the Royal Dee. In a way this is a pity, because Banffshire has both Highland and pastoral scenery. But for the visiting angler it may be an advantage — accommodation is easily found in the holiday months, and that is when sea trout are running.

I have had excellent fishing when staying at Huntly, where I fished the Deveron itself and two smaller rivers, the Isla and the Bogie. The Huntly Angling Association controls twenty-two miles of water and there is no problem getting a permit to fish, either for a day or a week or longer. The Castle Hotel has a private stretch for guests, with pools that are a joy to fish.

The local association water at Banff runs alongside the golf course and sea trout fishing there can be good, although so much depends on the run of the tide. The fish are usually more interested in bolting upstream to spawn at that early stage of their run. Permits can be obtained at the local tackle shop in the town.

My preference is for a more exclusive stretch of water farther up-river and I would recommend one of the hotel waters at Euchries, Bridge of Marnoch, or at Rothiemay. Mountblairy is now private but a day or two on that beat, if it can be arranged, is paradise.

For all my memories of that red letter day with the salmon, the Deveron to me spells sea trout; the big ones caught in the darkness of a summer night and fighting like living torpedoes.

Town of the three rivers (Deveron, Bogie, Isla)

Where else is there a small, neat town of pleasant people where a trip to the tackle shop or just along the street to the county hall, can buy a daily or a weekly permit for a few pounds to fish three splendid rivers to your heart's content for salmon, sea trout or trout? It's called Huntly, and it nestles in the rich farmland and pastured hills of inland Aberdeenshire.

Over its twisting length of forty-five miles the River Deveron has many fishing centres. There is Banff on the coast where the local angling association has about a mile of both banks of the tidal water. There are, of course, the well-known and prolific salmon and sea trout beats of Eden, Bridge of Marnoch and Mountblairy a few miles inland. Then there is the town of Turrif, in the heart of whisky country, with plenty of good fishing water. But it is in Huntly, I feel, that a visiting trout or sea trout angler can get all he would ever want, from the Deveron itself and its two main tributaries the Bogie and the Isla, both of which join it near the town.

These three rivers are called the Huntly Fishings and the twenty-two miles of river are controlled by the Fishings Committee in the town. On this stretch of the Deveron itself there are thirty-eight named pools and on the Bogie there are twenty-seven. So far as the Isla is concerned, there is a contrast between what some guidebooks would say about this stream and my own experiences with both sea trout and brown trout. The Isla seems to lack wonderful compliments but I can vouch for its excellence in producing some fine brown trout and, occasionally, some good sea trout.

For a river which, in 1966 during a public enquiry, was officially described as a first-class second-class salmon river, the Deveron has had its great moments in angling history in that part of north-east Scotland. In 1924, Mrs Morrison fished the Mountblairy beat with fly and caught a salmon of 62 lb. (Not far short of that one of 64½ lb caught by her sister-of-the-angle Miss Ballantyne on the Tay two years previously.) And the largest brown trout the river has produced is one of 10½ lb, caught by the keeper of the Ede beat, Mr W. Bain. Then he went on to land a sea trout of 14½ lb, probably a record fish for the river. Mr C. Sievewright caught a sea trout of 14 lb on the Inverechnie beat, and a brown trout of 7 lb was caught on the same beat with a Greenwell's Glory fly. This same water produced a sea trout of 8½ lb.

So much for the Deveron monsters. In the Huntly part of the river they allow clear water worming for trout and for sea trout. Whatever you or I might think of worming, there is no doubt that it works well here. It is not so easy, either. While it is one thing lobbing a worm into a current and hoping for the best, it is another thing altogether casting the worm in clear water upstream of the spot where you think a trout is lurking. And that is usually on the edge of the white water. There is nothing 'automatic' about the strike, either. You have to be pretty gentle in raising the rod and setting the hook once you know he is on, particularly if you are using a single hook.

The Bogie produces slightly bigger trout than the Deveron but the pinnacle of brown trout excellence can be reached where the two rivers join at Conniecleugh.

I have an angling friend, a dry-fly fanatic, who spends his entire summer holiday (he is a bachelor!) fishing the Isla about two miles outside Huntly. He takes his caravan up there and he is in heaven for two weeks. I have seen his catches and they are tremendous — fish of 2 and 3 lb among the scores of one-pounders and less.

Huntly indeed is in the heart of all this — three grand rivers, each with its own characteristic for trout anglers who like a challenge.

An angler's dream river in Scotland (Findhorn)

I know a river in Scotland that seems to have evolved from anglers' dreams. It is not particularly long, not particularly wide and certainly not particularly famous when compared with the Royal Dee, the glorious Spey or the magnificent Tweed. You may not have heard of it if you are a trout angler.

It rises in the wild mountain range behind Newtonmore where there are no roads but where there are enough salmon, grilse, sea trout, finnock and brown trout to gladden the heart of any angler who can reach those glorious pools and glides, to see them leap and rise and scurry to their feeding or their spawning grounds. From its source the river cascades, flows gently, roars through gorges then quietly whispers over gravel and pebbles on its way through every conceivable type of fishing water to the Moray Firth and the North Sea. The estuary here is a wide sea loch where thousands of sea trout and finnock rush in at every tide before the waters go through the Sahara of sand-dunes called the Culbin Sands.

Even the name seems to come from a distant Norse dream — the Findhorn.

The Findhorn comes from the Grey Mountains (that's the English translation of the Monadhliath range) and is formed by the confluence of two streams, the Eskin and the Cro. Then, fifteen miles downstream at Tomatin, it flows through some of the wildest, untamed moorland in Scotland, the sanctuary of red deer, grouse and wild goats. This heather-enfolded area is where most salmon spawn. Down again from Tomatin for some miles, the river passes lonely, ruined cottages and vestiges of bygone Highland villages till it reaches the bridge at Dulsie. Now it changes character and becomes a wild, thundering giant as it roars through the famous gorges which have characterised the area. A glimpse of those high precipices echoing the white thunder of the river below compels passing motorists on the road to Forres to stop and see the spectacle. The gorges are 200 feet high in places and so narrow that it is just possible for a very brave and physically fit person to leap from one edge to the other over the roaring torrent. This is why the most famous (or notorious) of these gaps is called Randolph's Leap, after the tale of a hunted soldier who fled the government troops during the 1745 rebellion. No other river in Scotland has such a spectacle as these

The road bridge pool on the Findhorn.

gorges. The 'Leap' is twelve miles south-east of Nairn, off the B9007 road.

After the Gorges, the Findhorn becomes quieter and is joined by various small tributaries, such as the Divie and the Dorback, flowing from Lochindorb, a good trout-fishing loch reached by an unclassified road off the A939 north-west of Grantown-on-Spey. Incidentally, on an island in this lonely loch there is a thirteenth century castle which was once the seat of the Comyns. It became the stronghold of the cruel and savage Earl of Buchan, who was called the 'Wolf of Badenoch' and who terrorised the area.

For the ten miles or so down to Forres, the water runs over gravel stretches and excellent fishing 'flats' that are interrupted by some very good salmon and sea trout pools. Then there is a tributary near Findhorn Bay by Broom of Moy village called the Muckle Burn ('muckle' is Scots for 'big'), which at one time was considered the best sea trout water on the Moray Firth. That was before water abstraction operations for agricultural purposes spoiled it for anglers.

The Findhorn frankly attracts more salmon anglers than sea trout or trout fishers. But for my part, the trouting on this dream of a river has given me well-remembered days in wonderful surroundings. Like most good Scottish salmon rivers — even the medium-sized ones — trout and sea trout fishing is often an underdeveloped potential. For those who prefer fishing for herling or sea trout the Findhorn is superb.

Getting permission to fish the river is not as easy as it is on many other east-coast rivers. Most of the estate beats upstream from Forres are privately held and, where they are leased, it is usually on long terms to the same people. For all this, there are two substantial areas I would recommend for the avid trouter.

The first is the part of the river around Forres. Permits and tickets are normally confined to the residents of the area but visitors are granted permission to fish if they stay in the district for a week. The price is around £30 and it is excellent value. Tickets are obtainable from the local tackle shop in Forres.

The local angling association controls this part of the water, which has sixteen excellent salmon pools and countless sea trout runs. The association is very strict about when, where and how an angler may fish. Poachers and other illegal or unsportsman-like fishers are given short shrift here. All this makes for a well-run angling river.

One of the reasons why association members take such pride in 'their' river is that many years ago they had a benefactor. He was a successful banker in New Zealand called Arthur Murdoch, who came originally from the village of Rafford, a few miles from Forres. In his will he left sufficient money to Forres Town Council to purchase or lease the fishing rights over this part of the Findhorn and the angling association has been managing these rights ever since. The 185 members see themselves as their own watchdogs and gamekeepers of the water.

The other area I would recommend for enthusiasts of the trout is at Tomatin. The Freeburn Hotel has a beat here which has some very good trout and fishing for them in April and May can be an unforgettable experience.

Near Forres, there is a very long and exciting pool called Anton's and it is here that I have had my best sea trout experiences. Regulars who fish it for sea trout are the many RAF people stationed at Kinloss and they were very helpful to me in selecting flies. I did best on small Teal and Silvers, size 12, or Cinnamon and Golds. Walking over the large stretches of pebbled banking can be sore on the feet but it is possible to get a car along the dirt road to within thirty yards of the pool.

Anton's, however, is only one of the many pools and glides on the Findhorn around Forres; every one has an exhilarating prospect for an angler who stays a week in this dream country.

Finnock from the Ugie

Before the turn of the century, the famous angling author Thomas Stoddart, in his *Angler's Companion*, wrote,

> 'The only other river in Aberdeenshire deserving notice is the Ugie which flows into the sea near Peterhead'.

Presumably he had fished and waxed eloquently about the other famous rivers the Dce, the Don and the Deveron.

Of course, he was correct in describing the Ugie as merely deserving some 'notice' if he meant salmon angling. The river has never been in the first league for fishing the King of Fish. Back in Stoddart's time, the main fishing on the river belonged to a Mr Arbuthnot, of

Although the salmon caught in the Ugie are sizeable and compare well, for such a small water, with those of Aberdeenshire's larger rivers, the numbers are never very high. Pitfour Fishings register seventy salmon and eight-five grilse for a year. The main sport, therefore, is for sea trout and finnock fishing.

Why is this? Some research into the nature of the Ugie taught me something about migrating

Collin's Pool on the Findhorn in Moray.

Logie Bank, and all he made from letting out the salmon beats was £45 per year. Even in those days of lower fishing rents this was hardly a bonanza for a riparian owner of a Scottish salmon river in the north east. Over the ten year period from 1900, the most salmon caught in any one year was forty-eight. That was in 1903. The following year they caught thirteen but — this is the significant point — in that same year, anglers caught 2,000 sea trout! The signs were there in those early fishing days, pointing to the Ugie as a first-class little sea trout river. By and large, that is what it is today.

fishing in Scottish rivers. The stages are easy to follow in terms of what nature does. On the Ugie, from Scott's Pool downstream to the sea, the water is quite shallow. The coast around the mouth of the river is very exposed and without shelter, which is hardly surprising; a look at the map shows how far that area of Buchan around Peterhead juts out in the North Sea. The autumn and winter storms ravage that coastline mercilessly, bringing tons of sand and gravel to the estuary of the Ugie. Most of the time the run of fresh water from the river cannot beat this onslaught, which means that bigger fish cannot get through the barriers of sand unless the tide is high enough, whereas sea trout and finnock have no such problems.

The district of Buchan in Aberdeenshire is rather flat with no prominent hills, the highest being the Hill of Mormound, which is 769 feet above sea level. The Ugie cuts its way through this somewhat plain land providing welcome scenic beauty to a countryside relieved only by remote farms and woodlands.

The river is really formed by two others which join — the North Ugie Water and the South Ugie Water. From the point where these two rivers meet, near the village of Longside, to form the main river, the distance until it reaches the sea is only six miles. North and South Ugies are sixteen and eighteen miles respectively, so the whole length of the river is twenty-four miles.

There must be something special about the Ugie today which I am missing. One of my good fishing companions in the north is Harry Munro, a well-known angling journalist and broadcaster in these parts. In summer and autumn, almost every time I telephone his home in Aberdeen, his wife tells me that Harry and his son are 'awa' fishin'. The questions I always ask are: do Harry and his son have some private Eldorado beat on the glorious Royal Dee at the behest of Majesty? Or on the Don? Or are they after those magnificent big sea trout on the estuary of the Ythan at Newburgh? After all, all these rivers are nearer Harry's home in Aberdeen. No. They are fishing the Ugie — right up there at Peterhead.

I think I know now what it is about this relatively small water which is so attractive. It is the sea trout and the finnock fishing, to say nothing of the resident brown trout lurking in the slower-moving water on the South Ugie. Finnock (virgin sea trout coming up to spawn for the first time) give superb sport at sunset.

Looking at the pools on the Ugie, from the mouth of the river where it enters the North Sea at Buchanhaven near Peterhead, the first is the Colley Burn Pool, which is quite close to the sea and has plenty of finnock during the season. The Colley Burn itself, which enters the main stream here, comes through a narrow valley from the Howe of Buchan. The next pool is Scott's Pool, a deep and dark section where salmon rest, but which fishes well for finnock if there is a good breeze to ruffle the surface, particularly in the evening. Below

Inverugie Bridge there is a pool, but above the bridge the water is broken for about a quarter of a mile and is ideal for sea trout and finnock fishing. After this comes the Meadow Pot Pool, then the Cruive Pot Pool and finally, overshadowed by the old ruins of Inverugie Castle, comes the longest pool on the river — Pot Sunken.

Inverugie Castle, incidentally, was built in the sixteenth century and by marriage came into the hands of the De Keths or Keiths (note the name of Keith, a small town not far away), who subsequently became the famous Earls Marischal. The last member of this family to own Inverugie Castle was caught up in the rebellion of 1715 and had to flee to Germany where he became a favourite of Frederick the Great.

Farther upstream is Ravenscraig Pool and Craig Pool, at one time recognised as the best on the river for fishing.

The Ugie Angling Association manages much of the fishings on the river and does it very well. Tickets for visitors to the area are available from tackle shops in Peterhead and from various hotels in the district of Buchan.

The little Ugie is a river without pretence. It does not put on the airs and graces of its bigger brothers in Aberdeenshire or gain for itself a reputation of being a major salmon river. It seems content to be the haunt of thousands of sea trout and finnock, to the delight of anglers who like to fish small and enjoy the thrill of those bars of silver.

Sea trout on the tide (Ythan)

Perhaps as an angler you have caught all you want of stew-pond-fed rainbows in reservoirs. Or you have had your share of dry-fly fishing on southern chalk streams. Or you are fed up with travelling miles to catch a salmon, only to face a drought and no fish. Sea angling is not for your stomach and you would rather leave coarse fishing to the competition men.

Perhaps you are ready for the Ythan.

If you are, then you must get used to the idea of one of the greatest challenges in game fishing and the idea of a living torpedo on the end of your line, on a water that has been described as the finest sea trout stretch in Europe. It is the estuary of the Ythan river at Newburgh.

I had not fished the Ythan until a few years ago when my old friend Harry Munro introduced me to it. And that is surprising because estuary fishing has always appealed to me since my excellent experiences on the North and South Esks and on the Spey near its mouth. Another reason why I like tidal stretches is that the fishing is not so dependent on rainfall as is the case farther upstream. Even in times of near drought the sport is fairly reliable, thanks to the tides. Conversely, this can be a draw-back because angling is confined to tide-times and on the Ythan estuary this means about five hours fishing during the ebb.

The River Ythan is in Aberdeenshire. It rises in the mountains in the Wells of Ythan and runs for thirty-five miles through magnificent Highland scenery to Newburgh, where it empties into the North Sea through a wide sandy firth about four miles long. The area is a nature reserve and bird sanctuary, and for the sea trout fanatic it is a Valhalla.

Newburgh is a neat village fourteen miles north of Aberdeen and anglers go there from all over Europe, particularly now that Aberdeen airport has daily services from London, Paris and Amsterdam. While there I met German and Swiss fishers as well as, of course, a few English anglers who know a good sporting bargain when the see it. The charge for fishing this six mile stretch of water with seventeen named pools was a few pounds per day.

Eddy Forbes, the fisheries manager, took me downstream to the estuary at the tide turn. Right away I was impressed. Easy wading on shingle and firm sand . . . gently-flowing water to carry the flies downstream . . . and the unmistakable evidence before my eyes of sea trout galore splashing and walloping around. They were plopping and crashing about all over the water.

Harry and I started fishing at 6 p.m. and with each passing half-hour the rising fish were

Fishing for Ythan sea trout at the turn of the tide.

increasing in numbers and — it seemed to me — in size. I had never seen so many sea trout on one stretch of river.

Catching them, of course, is another matter. Both fly fishing and spinning is permitted and I tried both. On the fly, a two-fly cast, I had a few hair-raising pulls after casting over the rings of rising fish, but they came to nothing. Either something was wrong with my striking or the fish took fright at the last split-second. Then I got a two-pounder and that felt as if it was a fish of three times that weight. If the salmon is the King of Fish, then I would describe these Ythan sea trout as the Warriors.

It was Eddy's special Ythan fly that took my sea trout — something like a Cinnamon-and-Gold pattern with a long, trailing tail-feather — although other anglers were doing just as well with reliable stand-bys. Most spinning anglers were using a Ythan Terror — a locally-made imitation minnow of blue and silver with some feathers on the end. As far as I could find out, there seemed to be little difference in catches between the fly fishers and the spinners.

This estuary area is called the Ythan Fishings and belongs to the Udny Estate. It is well managed by Eddy Forbes in co-operation with Newburgh Angling Club. River watchers come down heavily on anyone who is using bait or fishing illegally; poachers are firmly seen off the water, usually to the point of no return! Eddy supervises the commercial netting operation and the gauge of nets allows sea trout and immature salmon to get upstream, catching the mature salmon at specific times and within certain dates. This strict control improves the fishing for anglers every year and the sea trout population is now one of the best in Europe.

Udny Castle is in the centre of this beautiful Scottish Highland estate and dates from the thirteenth century. The house itself, although modernised to high standards, still retains its ancient charm. Cottages and stable flats surrounding the castle are let to holiday visitors. For estuary fishing at Newburgh, there are two excellent hotels and there are furnished caravans for visitors.

I suppose I spent too much time chatting to other anglers to concentrate on my own fishing. But it was worth it. Dr Hubert Zehnder with his two sons were there from Switzerland; as well as six sea trout, he caught two flounders on the fly! Fifteen-years-old Cameron Smith had caught eighty-six sea trout since the beginning of the season. Farmer John McNicoll was catching fish of 3 and 4 lb regularly and Eddy told me that ten-pounders are not uncommon. One man, a German from Frankfurt, had been fishing at Newburgh for ten years.

I may not share the German gentleman's persistence, but Eddy Forbes and my friend Harry Munro can be sure of one thing — I will go back to Newburgh.

Gannochy Bridge Pool on the North Esk.

A typical example of the wild plants to be found on the banks of the Spey.

The whisky river (Livet)

Someone once said there were so many whisky distillers up around Speyside that a drink from any of the streams would make you feel intoxicated. This is quite untrue, of course, but you could feel an intoxication of a non-alcoholic blend if you took a fishing rod through any of the Spey's wonderful tributaries.

I first had this exhilarating experience in the heartland of Scotland's Highlands many years ago, when I took one of the beats of the Richmond Arms Hotel in Tomintoul on the River Avon. I returned many times, though I was neither very skilful with the method used (single worm on large Stewart tackle hooks) nor very lucky with salmon. They cast into white water on this river and the salmon —

other people's that is — snatch the lure as it passes.

I had one grand day, however, on one of the two tributaries which run into the Avon before it, in turn, runs into the Spey at Ballindalloch. The two streams are the Conglass, which has mainly sea trout, and the Livet, which has both salmon and sea trout. The area has something else, a world-wide reputation for the distilleries that produce superb Glenlivet single malt whiskies.

John McNiven, the owner of the hotel, sent me up the Livet that July day and, taking his advice, I fished upstream using a single Blue Charm double-hooked fly. I cast into the rough water as if dry flying, lost two good sea trout and caught one.

This lovely, whisky-famed river runs near Tomintoul in the heart of the mountains and the fishing is managed by the hotel. I keep promising myself another trip to this magnificent county, and the sooner the better.

Tayside to The Coast

The rivers

Tay · Earn · South Esk · North Esk

A trout fisher on the River Tay in Perthshire.

The impertinent trout of the Tay

Trout on the Tay seem to have a life of their own. They are not in the least interested in the salmon which invade their areas. They have their own territorial problems, their own preference for flies, nymphs or worms, and they stick to what they know and like.

That such a species as the common brown trout has the impertinence to exist in Scotland's largest water catchment area and Scotland's premier salmon fishery, seems an absurd situation. In all of the 117 miles of that world-famous river, who on earth could understand the wishes of a dedicated trout angler?

Unlike fishing for the King of Fish, there is very little chuck-it-and-chance-it about trout fishing. Of course, this is not to say that a salmon fisher gambles wildly on every cast. But the signs he looks for are different. The height and flow of the water, the temperature, the

71

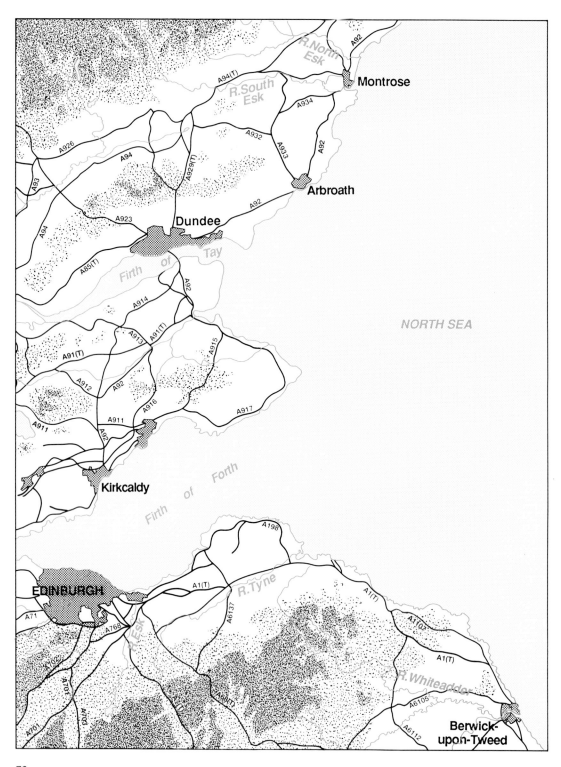

general weather conditions, the brightness of the day, and the knowledge of established lies, are some of the factors considered by a salmon angler. The trout fisher notes these, too, plus what his eyes are telling him when he sees the tell-tale rings on the surface of a smooth pool, and that is just the start of his challenge. Bait or fly? Upstream dry or downstream wet? Big flies or small ones? Into the white water or the smooth glide? At the neck of the pool or at the tail?

This much I do know about trouting the Tay with wet flies: unless the flies, particularly the tail one, are an exact replica of what the fish are feeding on at that time in that place, nothing will happen. But, oh the thrill! The sheer, electrifying, feeling of triumph when contact is made! The leader jolts, the line straightens out and the fight is on for one of Scotland's finest trout from Scotland's greatest angling river. In my experience, the flies best used on the Tay are sizes 12 or 14, though in big waters a size 10 might be better. Patterns

are the ever-faithful Greenwell's Glory and March Brown, Olive Quill, Blae and Black and Butcher. In summer, a floating line is most suitable.

Besides being Scotland's longest river, the Tay is many things — a culmination of many waters from a catchment area that is certainly Scotland's largest, draining 2,800 square miles. What we call the Tay starts life as a stream away up in Ben Lui, a mountain of 3,708 feet, eighty-five miles upstream from the tidal water at Perth. It begins as the River Cononish, receiving water from the burns around the village of Tyndrum, becomes the River Fillan, passes Crainlarich, enters Loch Dochart and Loch Lubhair. Now it becomes the River Dochart that flows down Glen Dochart and over the roaring Falls of Dochart, almost in parallel with the River Lochay where both of them enter Loch Tay joyously at Killin.

At the other end of the loch at Kenmore, the river comes out of the loch and is now the Tay proper. It runs in splendour past Taymount

The River South Esk near Edzell.

Castle and through some of the grandest wooded countryside in Britain. Colonel Thornton described this area of the Tay in 1896 in his book about a sporting tour through the Highlands:

> 'There certainly never was a more interesting assemblage of all the beauties of Alpine scenery, and the most finely-cultivated grazing farms . . . The features are so various, so noble and so majestic, that they surpass the art of the painter.'

From this point downstream the river is joined by the River Lyon and passes the village of Aberfeldy. Fifteen miles farther down it is joined by the Tummel at Logierait, flows down to Dunkeld near Birnham, is joined by the Braan and the Almond before it sweeps majestically past Scone Palace and the city of Perth. About seven miles farther down at Jamestown, the River Earn is the last major tributary to join the Tay as it sweeps thirty-one miles farther from Perth to Dundee and the sea.

There is trouting everywhere. In the lochs, burns and rivers of Tayside there are brown trout, sea trout and grayling. Coarse fish are also in abundance in the main river for those whose fancy takes them to slower waters. The famous salmon beats of Ballathie, Stobhall, Stanley and Scone, of course, have trout a-plenty but there are obvious reasons why few bother to fish for them. The high price a salmon angler pays for the privilege of fishing these well-known and prolific salmon stretches makes it somewhat foolish for him to set up a trout rod and go after smaller fish.

Not all the stretches, however, are in the high-price league, even for salmon, and there are good association and club waters which are run by the Aberfeldy Angling Club, the Dunkeld and Birnham Angling Association and the Perth and District Angler's Association. In addition, the local hotels at Dunkeld, Grandtully and Logierait all arrange trout fishing for guests.

The tributaries, too, have good trout fishing waters where permits are inexpensive and easily obtained by visitors from the various associations. The Tummel is a good example, where the Pitlochry Angling Club have five miles of both banks, from the junction of the Tay up to Pitlochry. The Atholl Angling Club has parts of the Garry and the Tilt, while the Strathmore Angling Improvement Association manage parts of the Isla and the Dean. They also have their own trout hatchery at Glamis. Blairgowrie, Rattray and District Angling Association handle fishing on the River Ericht.

It was no accident, or the stabbing of a pin on a map, that placed the Freshwater Fisheries Laboratory at Faskally in Pitlochry in 1948. This excellent organisation began life as the Brown Trout Laboratory to research Scottish brown trout, though most of its work now is with salmon. Its location is well chosen in the heart of this huge water catchment area.

There is another significant feature of the Tay and its many tributaries which is of interest to anglers. The whole drainage area is dammed and tunnelled in a complicated system for the generation of hydro-electricity. Although this vast operation, which began in the thirties, caused (and still causes) widespread adverse criticism among salmon angling interests, trout fishing seems to have been affected in a positive way and, for those who decide to forget salmon, there is really good sport in the main river and throughout the whole of Tayside.

In waters like the upper reaches of the Clyde, a trout angler knows he is in for few surprises; the fish that rise for his flies are trout and, in some cases towards the end of the season, grayling. In famous and prolific salmon areas such as the Tay, however, an angler fishing for trout may find himself having the most hair-raising experience of his life when a salmon of perhaps 15 lb snatches his tail fly. Then he has the classic problem of trying to control a salmon with trout tackle. His nylon leader has a breaking strain of 5 lb, the hook size of his fly is 10, yet the fish is firmly hooked and the reel is screaming as it dashes about all over the pool, perhaps into the rough water or into the next pool. A trout angler needs time, patience and great dexterity and needs to know just how much pressure he can put on the fish before he can hope to land it.

He needs something else; a very credible story to tell the water bailiff when he comes along and asks why a trout angler with a trout permit is standing over a 15 lb salmon!

The trout on the River Tay, in my opinion, promise a sport that demands greater attention and development. Of course, part of the problem is salmon fishing and the value of the higher-priced beats. But, as I have indicated, not every part of the Tay or its other rivers is valuable salmon water. There are trouting stretches above Perth, at Pitlochry and downstream from Dunkeld House Hotel which are a delight for any trout angler, and every encouragement should be given to the many angling clubs which manage such stretches. A river

after the last war, salmon anglers, riparian owners and fishing hoteliers have been complaining. That is the general impression I get every time I go to Balinluig, Pitlochry, or to Dunkeld.

Whatever the truth of the matter may be, whether hydro-electricity schemes have ruined

Hunting for the Tay's 'residents'.

with eleven major tributaries and three large lochs in its domain has the potential of being, apart from its salmon fishing, a paradise for the dedicated trout angler.

Thank goodness for the residents! (Tummel)

Ever since the hydroelectric people started monkeying around with the Tay river system

salmon fishing or not, there is hardly a grey-haired fisher or ghillie in this part of Scotland who has not remembered better days before the tunnelling and damming, pumping and channelling changed the waters. One river above all others has been mourned — the Tummel. This, like the Earn and the Lyon, has always been something more than a tributary of the mighty Tay. It is a river in its own right, all fifty-eight miles of it, from its birth in the mountains of the Black Mount deer forest above Loch Ba to where it joins the Tay at Logierait. The outlet of Loch Rannoch is the proper start of the river, because here it is as far from the source of the little Ba as it is from its junction with the Tay.

There is little doubt that some well-known

angling beats were wiped out by the reservoirs. Salmon spawning areas were flooded and now the fish are expected to react to the artificial rises and falls of river water instead of the natural results of rainfall. All this has had a negative effect on the fishing, some say irretrievably so. By contrast, the fish ladders at Pitlochry, to which thousands of visitors go every year, reveal through the spectator window salmon going up into Loch Kaskally and the spawning areas beyond. The metered numbers are very respectable. It all depends which pair of spectacles you use to examine the figures before you join the enthusiasts, or the critics of hydro-electricity. It is perhaps as well that the Freshwater Fisheries Laboratory is situated at Faskally near Pitlochry, as they research the situation year by year.

It is as well, too, that the Tummel, like its big brother the Tay into which it flows, has resident brown trout as well as migrating salmon which depend on variable water flows. Some of these 'permanent residents' grow to a considerable size and three or four pounders are not uncommon. The largest brown trout caught so far in the Pitlochry part of the river weighed 7½ lb.

The trout angler on the Tummel has great advantages. Access to the river from places like Kinloch Rannoch or Pitlochry is very good. The cost of permits to fish for trout only is absurdly low and contrasts widely with the permits for salmon. Indeed the Pitlochry Angling Club manages five miles of both banks of the river and the price of a daily ticket is less than that for two packets of cigarettes! The stretch is from the junction of the river with the Tay, right up to Pitlochry Dam. The limit for trout anglers is six fish per rod.

In this angler's paradise of Tayside — the largest catchment area in Scotland — an angler has a very wide choice of rivers and lochs. Although most of the attention is given to salmon, the brown trout fishing on the Tummel is a welcome relief. The scenery is magnificent and the opportunities for having a large stretch of water almost to oneself is high.

The Department of Recreation and Tourism of Tayside Regional Council publish a booklet entitled *Tayside: Scotland's Region of the Rivers* which gives detailed information about almost everything the trout fisher would want to know about all the waters in the region. The

River Tummel is well listed, showing how to get there, where to fish and at what cost for anglers.

Whatever critics might say of the changes affecting the salmon in the Tummel, trout anglers can be glad that the brown trout are still very much in residence.

Deadly for trout (Tay)

Can you imagine a river which is 117 miles long, with ten major tributaries that are rivers in their own right; with thousands upon thousands of excellent brown trout; where trout angling costs only a few pounds per day or per week; that flows through the most magnificent scenery in Scotland; that gives easy access to the best trouting stretches — yet is hopelessly underfished and its trout almost neglected?

When I tell you that this is the Tay river system you will understand why the brown trout is a potential Klondyke for game fishers. The salmon is King on the Tay and its feeding rivers. Little wonder. Beats are expensive, protection and keepering of the private stretches are outstanding and neither the salmon anglers nor their lessees nor ghillies have much time for the river's resident fish, the humble trout.

John Ashley-Cooper, in his book *The Great Salmon Rivers of Scotland*, mentions standing on Kinclaven or Caputh bridge and watching a big rise taking place as 'quite an experience'. Big fish of 4-6 lb are occasionally caught.

When I started fishing many years ago, I innocently fell in with a poaching incident on the Tay and it taught me a lesson, not about anglers, but about going on a trip with someone you do not know too well. His name was not Peter but that is what I will call him. He is dead now and I would hate his family's memory of him to be sullied by the tale.

I had barely learned to cast a line when Peter asked me if I would like to come with him to a good stretch of the Tay.

'Where?' I asked.

The Tay at Aberfeldy.

'Up around Dunkeld. It's a private bit.'

I knew enough about the private waters of the Tay and the difficulty in getting permission to fish them to ask, 'If it's private, how do we get permission to fish?'

'The gamekeeper's a pal of mine. There'll be no charge.'

'Will he be there?' I did not fancy the prospect of some invisible gamekeeper nodding his approval to Peter and me from afar, then leaving us to the tender mercies of some other river watcher who might hand us over to the local police.

'Of course he will. We will call at his cottage which is almost on the river bank. Does that satisfy you?'

'Okay'. I felt better.

We got to the river mid-morning. We met the gamekeeper who confirmed the arrangement.

'Remember,' he said, 'It's trout you're fishing for — nothing else.'

'Of course,' Peter said, and I nodded enthusiastically. 'Just trout.'

'All right,' he said, 'Off you go.'

We drove the car down a shingly road to a little riverside beach which looked a veritable paradise for easy wading and wonderful trout fishing by wet fly. The river was big at this part and flowed steadily and unbroken right down the whole span till it turned in a wide bend towards the trees.

I could hardly wait to get my rod assembled and Peter was just as keen to get started. I would like to be able to say that we filled a basket with the one and two pounders for which the Tay is famous. We did nothing of the kind. I could excuse myself for not catching fish because I was a novice and this was only my second time on a river. But Peter could not excuse himself.

'We're using the wrong flies,' he said, when we were having our sandwich-and-coffee lunch on the bank. 'Up here on the Tay you have to be dead right with the flies you use – specially the trout fly.' He poked his way through his fly-box.

'What'll you try now?'

'I'm going to give them the Black Pennel on the tail. If that doesn't take them, I'm beat.'

'What should I tray?'

'Oh — anything. Here — try this. 'He held out what I now know was a Teal and Green, size 12.

I got the first trout, a fine fish weighing about a pound. Peter thrashed the water upstream from me but rose nothing. He was tight-lipped but managed a congratulatory smile when I landed my second trout.

At about three in the afternoon Peter's patience was gone; I caught no more fish — particularly for his peace of mind — and we splashed our way on to the pebbled bank.

'What now?' I asked.

'There's only one thing — a wee Mepp.'

'What's that?'

He was assembling his spinning rod. 'A little wobbler. Bright silver.'

'But that's spinning.'

'So?'

'I thought it was fly only.'

He fastened the little Mepp spoon on to the nylon. 'He said *trout* only.'

'Oh.'

'So — here we go.' He stomped down over the gravel and waded into the water while I watched him. It was the first time I had seen a spinning rod in action as Peter cast the Mepp right over to the far bank.

It was the first time for me for something else — seeing the rod bend over, hearing Peter's cry of triumph, seeing him dig the butt of the rod into his stomach as the reel of the rod reverberated in frantic up-and-down movements. I heard his reel whine and I knew what had happened. He was into a fish.

He landed it after quarter-of-an-hour of grunting and panting and, again for the first time in my life, I witnessed a salmon being netted as Peter, glowing with pride, hoisted the fish in the net up to the pebbles. He delivered the *coup de grâce* and sat down to admire the fish. Then he weighed it with a little hooked scale.

'Sixteen and a bit,' he said.

'Pounds?'

'Yes'.

'But you can't take it.'

He looked at me. '*Can't* take it? Can't take it where?'

'Home'.

He stared at me. 'What d'you suggest I do with it? Throw it back?'

'We'll have to tell the gamekeeper at least.'

'We'll have to do nothing of the kind. C'mon.' he led the way to his car, opened the boot and laid the fish in it, covering it carefully with a large tartan rug. Then he put all our fishing gear — haversacks, waders, coats etcetera, on top.

I didn't know what to say. Then as we drove up the little road to the gamekeeper's cottage, I said 'I'm an accessory.'

'Yes, you are.'

'Suppose he . . .'

'Suppose nothing. You stay in the car — I'll do the talking. Where are your two trout?'

'Here.' I fetched them in the plastic bag from the rear seat.

'Good. Let's have them.'

I felt myself perspiring and my face turn white and cold as I saw Peter chatting to the gamekeeper, taking my two trout from the bag and showing them with pride. Then they shook hands and we were off.

After a while, Peter was the first to speak. He had a big grin on his face. 'Didn't I tell you that the Tay's a great trout river. In fact it's the best trout river in Scotland if you ask me.'

I tried not to smile. 'I must remember that. What was that little tune you were whistling?'

'A wee Mepp. Deadly for trout.'

'Absolutely.' I laughed with him.

But why brown trout on the Tay?

There must be a reason why some rivers like the Tay with large salmon runs, are sparse on sea trout but have an excellent brown trout population. Conversely, other rivers like the Border Esk have grand runs of sea trout and finnock but also have a respectable salmon population. The Dee and the Don empty into the North Sea barely a mile or so from each other in Aberdeen yet, in their fishing stretches upstream, they are as different as chalk from cheese. The Dee has salmon in abundance but virtually no brown trout; at least, it is almost impossible to get permission to fish for them if they are there! On the other hand, the Don has reasonable and increasing runs of salmon; in addition, the brown trout fishing is famous all over the country. The latest speculation given to me recently, in all seriousness by a very experienced angler, is that the fishery owners on the river electrocute all the brown trout and get rid of them!

I have talked of these differences with many angling experts and even some academics, and have been offered many explanations. The most attractive one is the simplest — that sea trout do not like to travel very far away from salt water and they probably confine their spawning to the lower reaches of a river and the small streams there. It sounds plausible but then I think of the sea trout I have caught in parts of rivers many, many miles from an estuary, like, for instance, the Annan.

Another explanation on offer is that some rivers, like the Ugie in Aberdeenshire, empty into the open sea and, during late autumn and winter storms, the unprotected mouth of the river tends to get silted up with sand and gravel. The larger fish, the salmon in particular, cannot surmount this barrier to get into the river, whereas the smaller sea trout can. Thus — more sea trout than salmon. This is very interesting but does not explain the large sea trout frequently caught on the Spey in the lower reaches. Did they hitch a lift over the very open mouth of the river at Spey Bay?

Yet another suggested reason concerns the rate of flow of the river and the fact that larger and stronger salmon can overcome fast currents, whereas the smaller sea trout cannot. Again, this apparently takes no account of some salmon and some sea trout which are about the same weight and have possibly the same agility and strength. Nor does it explain how a river like the Dee can have a fast current all along its entire length.

Whatever the reason, all this does not explain the absence or presence of resident brown trout in a river. Obviously the avail-ability of food is paramount, but in some rivers where food is abundant and salmon abound, there are plenty of brown trout and virtually no sea trout. Yet, unlike salmon in fresh water, sea trout are voracious feeders.

It is this last combination which is very pertinent to the Tay and the one which is remarked on by many anglers on that river. There seems to be no obvious reason why there are so few sea trout in one of Scotland's most famed fishing rivers, a river which, with its many tributaries, is reckoned to produce around 12,000 salmon and grilse by rod and line every year. One reason which might apply particularly to the Tay is that the water is so huge — to say nothing of the tremendous sheet of water in Loch Tay — that the sea trout simply get 'lost' and do not come upstream in identifiable shoals. Yet another reason given is that the commercial nets catch most of them. This I doubt. Economics suggest that commercial netters are in the main business of catching salmon and not sea trout.

It is easier to understand why the wild brown trout on the Tay are not sought by anglers in great numbers. The keepers and the ghillies who have responsibilities for the salmon fisheries on the important beats of the river naturally have no great interest in the trout.

On the other less valuable parts of the river trout fishing is very popular among local anglers, even on Sundays when salmon fishing is prohibited but trout fishing is not. Of course, some salmon enthusiasts who fish on the Tay are always associating dubious motives to these trout anglers who find it necessary to use heavy breaking-strain nylon casts and remarkably large trout flies!

In consideration of why some rivers have a higher population of one kind of fish than another river, I often wonder if we anglers over-complicate such questions when trying to get answers. The most sensible remarks on the subject were made to me by two scientists at the Freshwater Fisheries Laboratory near Pitlochry. They had no hesitation in offering a simple explanation, namely, that each type of freshwater fish (salmon, sea trout and brown trout) will inhabit the water which suits it best for feeding and spawning. Trout (including sea trout) like slower water than salmon and like to keep in pools.

Yes, all very well, but . . .

A day on the Earn

For all the times I have fished that friendly, gratifying river, the Earn in Perthshire, I really had to wait until one August day to understand much about the river; not all of it, mark you, but enough to reinforce my opinion that this forty-six-mile-long water in the heart of the best of Scotland's scenery has almost everything a trout, sea trout or grayling angler could want.

The man who spent that day with me was John Shields, of the Crieff Angling Club, which manages about ten miles of the river for anglers. I first met John a couple of years previously when I taped an interview with him for a regular Saturday morning broadcast on fishing for the BBC. I was most impressed then with his knowledge of the river and his expertise as an angler.

First, a few facts about the Earn. You should understand right away that it is a tributary of the Tay at its lower end and, as such, is therefore part of the largest water catchment area in Scotland. This country has nothing bigger than this river system and, in my opinion, nothing is more prolific in game fish than this area of moorland, mountain and farmland in the heart of Scotland. You might say it is Scotia's Lower Highlands, splendidly steeped in legend and history, part of Sir Walter Scott's romantic prose. The mighty Tay has many famous tributaries well known to anglers: the Dochart, Lochay, Lyon, Tummel, Garry, Tilt, Isla, Ericht, Almond and this most southerly one, the Earn, which joins the Tay at Jamesfield, seven miles downstream from the city of Perth.

It is only when you look at the map of this part of Scotland that you come to realise the Earn 'missed it' by a few miles south-west of Perth. If there had been no mighty Tay . . . As it is, the salmon and sea trout come through

A fine catch from the Earn.

the Firth of Tay, past Dundee and under the Tay Bridge; some take the high road through Perth and go up to the wonderful beats of Stanley and Grandtully, which cost a great deal of money to fish. Others take the low road into the Earn, through the Bridge of Earn, through Forteviot, under Kinkell Bridge, past the town of Crieff and up to Loch Earn.

I have often thought that but for a few miles of unimposing land, the beautiful Earn might have been the majestic Tay.

Some people say that the Earn is a river in its own right and not strictly a tributary at all because of its size and the direction it takes. They may be right, but it does come under the jurisdiction of the Tay District Salmon Fisheries Board. The river rises at Loch Earn which gets its water from various small streams in the hills, mainly from the Ogle, which enters the loch at Lochearnhead.

Along the Earn there are about forty riparian owners of fishing stretches and a few angling clubs or associations — Auchterarder, Crieff, Dunning, Perth and Thistle. The part of the river I would like to describe is the area belonging to Crieff Angling Club.

It would be foolish to suggest that the Earn is primarily a river for the trout or sea trout angler. It is a salmon river. As part of the Tay system, how could it be otherwise? The Earn is the first of the tributaries the fish encounter. For all its fame for salmon, the river gives excellent sport with sea trout and, to a lesser extent, with brown trout. And I know personally of its bounty of 1 and 2 lb grayling because I have caught them at the back end of the summer at Forteviot and Comrie. A book I picked up recently suggested that brown trout fishing on the Earn was not at all significant. Significant or not, the trout on this river are there all right, usually lurking in the deeper holes under trees and bushes of which there are many on this river. Recently one of my friends took one on the fly and the trout weighed 2½ lb.

From late June until the end of July there is usually a big run of sea trout and the average weight of them is 1½ lb, although it is not unusual for sea trout of 4 or 5 lb to be caught.

I wonder whether other keen anglers who write about their experiences occasionally suffer my kind of humiliation?

Perhaps it is the destiny of all angling writers and broadcasters not to catch fish when they are in full view of an audience. It has happened to me too often *not* to give me embarrassment. There I am on a river, or out in a boat on a loch, and my watchful companions are thinking, 'Well, he *says* a lot about fishing on the radio and he writes a lot about it. Now let's see if his creel is bigger than his mouth.' And the result is usually nothing.

Conversely, my few red-letter days are usually when no one is around to see me take three sea trout in an hour from a sunset-purple river on a summer's evening. I am usually alone when fish on a loch are rising to every cast I make, or when my salmon rod bends into a fourteen-pounder at a thundering, white-foamed pool. I was once being recorded for television on the Aberdeenshire Dee with a famous personality and for two whole days neither of us caught anything, in spite of the fact that salmon were rising head-and-tail all around us.

The day I broke this evil spell was that day on the Earn with John Shields. Rod in hand, I waded out into a long, smooth, gravel-bottomed part of the river while he remained on the bank with camera poised.

'It's a good job you're just posing and not fishing.'

'Oh? Why's that, John?' I called, peeling off line from my reel.

'That's no place for trout on a day like this.'

I peeled off more line and let my three wet flies gently kiss the water and drift to the end of the glide before the rough water started. 'There's a fish behind that stone. I saw it rise.'

'You'll be lucky!' He was aiming the camera. Bang!

Yes, it was quite a trout. I brought it in gently, released it to the river and turned to John. 'Did you get the picture?'

'Yes. What did it take?'

'A Dunkeld. Size 12.'

That was indeed my day for beating the no-fish gremlin. An hour later we were again at a pool and each of us in the same role, John pressing the camera trigger and me fishing.

'I think there's one under those trees on the far bank.' I called

'That's a favourite spot but you'll never cast under these branches. You'll get hung up. Everybody does.'

I did cast sideways under the trees. I did not get hung up. The trout took my Dunkeld on the tail of my cast. And this time it was a fish of about 1 lb which I put back.

The business of rainbow trout escaping from a fish farm in the upper stretches of the Earn worries most trout anglers. An accidental 'escape' is one thing, it can happen on many rivers which have a fish farm on its reaches as, for example, on the Annan at Johnstonebridge. Altogether different are the instances of deliberate sabotage and that, John told me, is what happens. Poachers wearing wet suits get down under the water to the nets at the fish farm, cut them, and allow thousands of fish out into the river.

The rainbows make their way downstream because the way of these fish is to reach sea level sooner or later. On their way, they voraciously eat anything edible in sight and this includes fish eggs, and salmon and sea trout parr. It also means they compete — very successfully when we consider their growth rate — with the resident brown trout and with migrating sea trout for food. When twenty members of the Crieff Angling Club on the Strowan Beat were recently fishing in a brown trout competition, they landed only one brownie but a considerable number of rainbows. Nature, however, is wonderful in her capacity to compensate. A year after this incident, the members of St Fillan's Angling Club farther upstream caught forty trout while fishing the loch and there were only three rainbows among them.

My day with John on the Earn was a wonderful one and I am quite sure that the other thirty-six miles of the river which I did not visit were every bit as varied and promising as those beats we walked — the Drummond Castle Beat and the Strowan Beat.

The Esks

It would be a great pleasure to assure sea trout anglers how easy it is to get permission to fish the North Esk. That is, one of the two rivers in Angus, not the other two elsewhere in Scotland. Certainly the main owner of the fishing rights, the firm of Joseph Johnston, is a well-intentioned company which aims to maintain good relations with the communities around Montrose where its headquarters are — and

The Bridge of Dun stretch of the South Esk river.

that very much includes anglers. And it must be said that the only time I asked for a permit to fish a stretch of the river, I got it at once, without quibble, for the one-mile area of Morphie — and without charge! The ticket entitled me to fish from Denmouth of Morphie to Kinnaber Bridge, and I was lucky enough to get two good sea trout, taken on a Black Zulu in the white water by day. Only four permits are issued on any one day. None is issued in the month of May in order to allow salmon stocks to develop.

Day tickets are also available, costing from £5 to £20 on the Gallery and Canterland Beats. The Montrose Angling Club, or any of the larger Montrose hotels, will give good advice, as will the Montrose fishing tacklist. Short-term tickets elsewhere on the river are not easily obtainable but some beats can be leased.

Fishing anywhere you please on the thirty-odd miles of the North Esk is not possible. This is a pity, for the sea trout aficionados. Where else on this part of the Angus coastline are we to find such wonderful sea trout water or finnock bonanzas from the two Esks — the North and the South. (The word 'Esk', by the way, means nothing more complicated than 'water'.)

Both of these Esks in Angus are within a few miles of each other, running almost parallel on the way to the North Sea, and they enter the ocean four miles apart. The North Esk empties through sand-dunes three miles north of Montrose. In my opinion, what makes this river unique is the breathtaking scenery upstream along its course: rich meadows, glorious woodlands and colourful heather moors encompass the river for miles. Around The Burn above Edzell there are spectacular gorges. Through Glenesk the countryside is wild and Highland in prospect and in the autumn it is ablaze with purple heather.

The North Esk, as an angling river, has had more than its fair share of debits and credits over the years since the end of the last war. The District Fishery Board, working with Joseph Johnston and others, deserve much of the credit for blasting the steep falls or loops in the lower reaches of the West Water, the most important tributary, thus permitting migrating fish access to the spawning areas upstream. Other improvements have been originated or motivated by Johnston's, including the instal-lation of an automatic fish-counting apparatus at Kinnaber.

On the debit side, water is abstracted from Loch Lee up near the source and gas pipelines have damaged spawning areas and nursery beds. But the most important debit has been the illegal drift netting taking place off the Angus coast that affects the estuary fish. It is also quite evident that this part of the coastline is the most heavily netted in Scotland.

On balance, however, the river more than survives as an excellent fishing water, for sea trout in particular. Indeed it always seems to have been in the top rank. Robert Blakey, in his book, *The Angler's Guide to Rivers and Lochs of Scotland*, published in 1854, states that the coast fishings of the North Esk were at one time 'very valuable', and, including those of the river, brought a rental of £3,591. And in these fishings, 3,000 salmon, grilse and sea trout have been taken *in one day*.

I met a farmer in the Angus area a few years ago who bought a castle, put in central heating, then sold it at a considerable loss. The castle was 300 years old and he certainly improved it. After he had invested his money in the improvements, he found that he could not sell it, so he let it go for a few thousand pounds.

'What did you do *that* for?' I asked.

'I just bought it to get the fishing on the North Esk.'

'Was it worth it?'

'Not half! Best sea trout stretch on the whole river.'

'You'd be able to recoup all your loss — I mean by letting it out.'

'Why would I want to do that? I've certainly no intention of hacking down trees and bushes and cutting footpaths and erecting fishing huts and employing heaven knows how many river watchers and keepers. Not me.'

'What d'you want the fishing for?'

'Me.'

'Just you?'

'Right. A mile of it. Why not? All I've wanted all my life is my own salmon and sea trout stretch on this river. Now I have it. And it was worth every penny — even the loss I made on the castle.'

I suppose you have to be an angler to understand that kind of thing. I fished his stretch and for the first time in my life I got a taste of what it is like to wander down the banks of a magnificent river without another soul in sight and to cast away with rod and line and explore every run and every pool till I felt that electrifying jerk of a big fish that had been lying there in the rough water waiting for me. I suppose in a way it is like owning your own golf course — you are competing all the time with the most formidable rival you will ever find — yourself.

For all that the South Esk runs within a few miles of its sister river the North Esk, it is a slightly different kind of water. It rises only a few miles west of the source of the Isla, which is one of the main tributaries of the Tay. This is in the Grampian Mountains at Cairn Bannoch. Then it descends 3,000 feet through beautiful Glen Cova for seventeen miles to Cortachy Castle, where it is joined by a main feeder, the Prosen Water. For another twenty miles it continues to Montrose Basin where it is tidal and empties into the sea. The Noran Water is the only other tributary of similar size to the Prosen: it rises in Glen Ogil and enters the main river between Tannadice and Brechin.

One reason why the South Esk is such a good sea trout river (some say better than the North Esk) may well be the fact that it runs into Montrose Basin. And sea trout take to estuarial waters better than salmon.

Finnock fishing in spring at the tidal area of the river down from the Bridge of Dun is an experience I have enjoyed, thanks to the hospitality of the Montrose Angling Club. We fished that April day with little double-hooked flies, Bloody Butchers, Greenwell's and Teal and Silvers, and had an offer at nearly every cast. The finnock were plump fish of ¾ lb.

Another experience I have had, slightly up-river but still in the tidal zone, was fishing in the deep sunset for a big sea trout. The timing for this has to be just right — the right place at the right time of evening and at the right tide-time. It can be a little stressful when you feel the water rising around your knees, then up to your thighs and it is near darkness and you want to linger just a few minutes more to cast out to where you see the lilac-silhouetted rings of a big fish. This is night sea trout fishing at its best; casting flies over the 'plop' of a feeding fish . . . gently letting them drift in the slow current . . . then feeling the pull . . . the line straightening . . . and as you raise the rod you have a fight on your hands to keep the strain on the fish while reminding yourself that the sea trout with its soft mouth could break free any second.

Although the fishing on the South Esk is mostly private, the South Esk Estates office in Brechin let out a two-and-a-half mile stretch. Forfar Angling club have a stretch and may sell a permit to visitors. House of Dun Hotel has a very good beat available to hotel guests. Kirriemuir Angling Club has all of seven miles on the river and allows permits to visitors; the Ogilvy Arms Hotel has three miles of private water for which permits can be obtained.

Strathclyde

The rivers

Clyde · Machrie · Echaig

The Duneaton Water, a tributary of the Clyde above Crawfordjohn.

Valhalla on the Clyde

I had never fished before when I first cast a line in the Clyde twenty-five miles up-country from Glasgow.

I had returned from the war and got married. That summer my wife and I went on a country holiday to a small village called Roberton in South Lanarkshire. It was a delightful place on the edge of moorland with its own little church,

a little mill and a wonderful old-fashioned manor house called Marionton owned by two spinster ladies, the Misses Brown, whose father had been the local dominie in a school over the hill.

I had not thought about the Clyde, certainly not about that river of noise and bustle we knew in Glasgow, nor had I considered that the river had to start somewhere. Here it was, in this pleasant rolling country sweeping down from the lowland hills. On our way there by bus, I barely noticed the water when we crossed the bridge at Symington. I suppose I would not have thought about fishing either if it had not been for the Misses Brown's brother Wilfie, who came up every Friday from Glasgow for the weekend. After dinner he put on his waders and got together his rod and tackle.

'Where are you off to?' I asked when I saw him tackling up.

'Down the river.'

'Fishing?'

He grinned and I thought he was about to say, 'No, I'm playing the trombone,' because Wilfie was a bit like that. But what he said changed my life. 'Want to come?'

We went through the fence and across the fields. And there in the rose-coloured June evening we were on the edge of the quietly-gurgling river. The soft, faraway clouds were reflected in a pool as wide as a small loch and Wilfie and I stood there silently, me in waders too large and he in his old-fashioned chest waders and tackety boots. We watched the water and the rings of feeding trout as the circles slid quietly downstream to disappear in the white-scarved roughage.

'What do we do?' I asked.

'Do what I do but keep clear of my casting.'

Things might have been very different if I had not caught a fish that evening. It would simply have been an experience in the lilac hush of a riverside; I would have watched Wilfie as he wielded his rod with dexterity and hooked three fish and that would have been that.

But I caught two fish. And I was hooked. I could talk about little else as we walked across the field in the soft summer darkness to the village. I was seduced. The Clyde was mine and I was the river's.

It was some years later before my wife, family and I became constant weekend residents in the area. We bought a cottage at Elvanfoot (for which I paid £600!) and with it came the fishing rights on the Clyde at our back door. I remember that our annual feu duty came to twopence which was collected by a diligent lady from the Earl of Home's estate.

Oh, that pool by the little footbridge behind our cottage! It was teeming with some of the

A favourite fishing haunt on the Clyde, near Roberton.

largest trout I have ever seen. Most of them congregated in the evenings just where Elvan Water runs into the main river and many of them fed on flies from the trees on the opposite bank.

The scene around that entire part of the Clyde has not changed much today. The Daer Water still runs into the larger river about a mile upstream from Elvanfoot and the trout there are a dry-fly fisher's dream. The Elvan still gurgles its way down from the Leadhills and most summers there are still some holiday gold-hunters who pan the water for a gram or two of the pure, white, metal that was used to make a brooch for Her Majesty when she opened the Daer Reservoir in the fifties.

From the Telford Bridge, where the Elvanfoot road meets the A74, the river sweeps out in a wide curve to embrace wild, lonely country before turning in towards Crawford. In this curve lurk the big trout — some say as heavy as 10 lb — that are waiting for the right angler with the right tackle.

From Crawford downstream to Abington is the ideal trouting water that has delighted generations of fishers for a hundred years; indeed it was in Abington that this twenty-odd miles of a fishery was started by Matthew MacKendrick and William Robertson who formed an association to manage the waters. You can still see the monument to the memory of Matthew on the west bank of the river just outside Abington.

From here the river meanders through fields, alongside woods and through moorland, spreading itself invitingly in embracing pools for the angler. The best known of these is the famous Roberton pool, just where the Roberton Burn enters the river and where I was first seduced and caught by those trout on a June evening.

It would be difficult to find a more attractive river for the dedicated trout fisher. Perhaps it is a little over-populated at weekends but this is hardly surprising. So far nothing else has come along to mar this Valhalla. After a hundred years, the fact that salmon are frequently seen in the river's lower reaches at Glasgow can do nothing but make the prospect of the up-country Clyde one of the great fishing rivers in Scotland.

Fishing Clyde

My honeymoon with the Clyde and its trouting has lasted for over thirty years. It began the day I bought a cottage beside the little footbridge that spanned the infant river at Elvanfoot. At the foot of our garden we had a trout stream and pool that anglers dream about. From that point to twenty miles down-stream the Clyde is still a trout fisher's paradise. The whole river, from its source to the Tail of the Bank, is about fifty miles long.

But it is that twenty-mile stretch of trouting water which captivates me and anyone else who wades it with rod and line. Those travelling by train or car can see quite plainly the rippling waters of the Clyde and its tributaries snaking through the moors and farmlands of some of the loveliest lowland scenery in Scotland, before the river broadens in its industrial cradle to become what was once the majestic waterway of a thousand ships at Glasgow and beyond.

From the headwaters, where Elvan and Daer Waters meet just above 'our' cottage, through Crawford, Abington, Roberton, Thankerton, Symington, right down to Carstairs and even as far as Motherwell, the Clyde and its trout have been formally managed as a fishery since 1887, all that time developing access and conservation to a very high standard. Today this management is undertaken by what may well be the best organised angling body in Scotland, the United Clyde Angling Protective Association Ltd, whose members stock the river regularly from its hatcheries at Rigside and Abington.

I am the first to admit to bias about trout fishing on the Clyde. But I am not alone. It is said that the famous Scottish patriot William Wallace fished the Clyde and since his day, in the reign of King Edward (the Hammer of the Scots), countless anglers have 'cut their teeth' on the challenges of the Clyde fish. Clyde trout are very wary, elusive and 'educated', perhaps because of the clear waters and the high population of anglers over the years. This has brought about the evolution of special Clyde-style trout flies. They are sparse in dressing, lacking in colour (with the possible exception

The Stonebyres stretch of the Clyde.

of the Butcher) and are tied on small, fine hooks. Fishing-tackle shops in Glasgow and in the small towns of Clydesdale — Hamilton, Wishaw and Motherwell etcetera — know exactly what to recommend to anglers who want to 'fish Clyde'.

Twenty-odd miles of trouting water on *any* river would be difficult to discuss in generalizations. Indeed, I know some rivers in Scotland on which fishing generalities can hardly be made from one mile to the next. The Clyde, however, is different in this connection. From my own experiences, and that of many other Clyde anglers, I know that there are general conditions which seem to prevail right through the whole of the trouting area. When the wind comes from the east, for instance, fishing is invariably poor and one may as well go home. Fishing downstream with wet flies in the gloaming during June and July can be a tremendous experience, and the trout are usually bigger. When night fishing, anglers 'in the know' use the 'big, black flees' — in sizes

10 or 8 with no colour. On blustery days early in the season, they fish the white water. On calm, warm days, they wait till sunset and fish the ends of the pools. And at times like these they wade quietly and stay still.

Of course, contradictions and rumours and exaggerations are renowned; every pub from Lanark up through Biggar and Lamington has its quota of tall-tale-tellers. As far as size is concerned, the average weight of trout caught is around ¾ lb, though it must be said that trout weighing over 10 lb lurk in some deep holes, particularly in those stretches well downstream where there is competition from pike. In the pool behind Crawford village some years ago a boy caught a trout of 8½ lb! My biggest fish from the Clyde was one of 2 lb caught at Abington, although I confess to my line being broken a few times by fish far heavier than this.

The proximity of the river to industrial and coal-mining areas (only twenty-odd miles away) has for many years brought dedicated men and boys to fish the waters with worm, maggot, gadger and, of course, artificial flies. I met many of these anglers years ago when they came upstream to the river at our cottage. All of them were expert; they were 'Clyde fishers' and they fished fairly, seldom coming off the water without a full bag. When fishing wet fly downstream they usually had four flies on the cast and they never fished with bait unless it was really 'bait water' running full. The dry-fly man, too, was a joy to watch as he targeted his own home-made 'flee' upstream in a long, straight cast directly above a tell-tale 'ring' on the water, one that you or I might hardly see.

The days of angling coalminers and steel-workers on the Clyde are over now but their places have been taken by fishers from all over this part of west Scotland, and they come from all walks of life.

The rivers Clyde and Tweed both rise from one hillside. The Tweed flows east but the Clyde goes west, past Beattock Summit, round the top of the Daer Valley Reservoir, then down to Elvanfoot and villages down-river such as Lamington and Roberton. Then it swerves eastward through the Biggar valley — almost on nodding acquaintance with the Tweed at Broughton — before turning west again below Symington.

As far as trout angling is concerned, the Big Break in the Clyde happens at the spectacular waterfalls of Bonnington, Stonebyres and Cora Linn just above the village of New Lanark. The river there changes its character as it runs through the fruit-growing, garden-like areas of Kirkfieldbank and Crossford towards Hamilton, Wishaw and Motherwell. Not many people realise that the Clyde was once a major salmon river in Scotland and that Glasgow began its life mainly as a salmon-fishing village. For over a hundred years no salmon were seen in the river, until a few years ago as a result of the clean-up inspired by the Clyde River Purification Board. Salmon are now returning in small numbers. It had always been imagined that migrating fish could never get over the falls at New Lanark. Now the River Board are planning ahead and are confident that fish ladders could solve that problem.

Back to trout fishing. My own experiences with a fly rod have been most enjoyable where the tributaries enter the main river, at the mouths of the Potrail Water, the Camps, the Daer and the Duneaton. One of the most popular spots among anglers is where the Roberton Burn joins the river at the village of Roberton.

Permits for visitors who want to fish various stretches of the Clyde on the upper parts, 20-odd miles or so from Glasgow, can be obtained without trouble from fishing tacklists and hotels all the way along the river's route at Lanark, Biggar, Carstairs, Symington, Abington or Crawford. And, of course, tacklists in Glasgow also sell tickets. The prices for the various stretches are moderate; they cost only a few pounds for the day or for the week.

For all my love and fond memories of that part of the Clyde at Elvanfoot, my advice today for any visiting angler looking for easy wading and a great challenge with the most cunning trout in Scotland, would be to visit the Lamington area, which can be reached comfortably from the delightful small town of Biggar.

The watchdogs of the Clyde

Believe it or not, there are still some people who think that if a river is simply left to nature, it will somehow become populated with fresh-water fish of all kinds. People with these opinions come from various groups, even environmentalists, who should know better.

What is so often forgotten is that man is part of this thing called 'nature'. And, sadly, he has, too often, brought to the big water arteries of the world the worst pollutant and predatory practices in his struggle for economic survival.

Whatever, or whoever, causes a river to become fishless and barren, you may be sure it is not the angler. On the contrary, he has often been the saviour of some of the waterways in Britain that were turgid sewers for years.

It would be a disservice to trout anglers, particularly in Scotland, if tributes were understated, especially to those lovers of the sport who took on the almost impossible task of converting 30 miles of the most important river in Scotland into a trout fisher's paradise. These people were not of one generation. They did this for a hundred years — grandfathers, fathers and sons — until today their association is possibly the most successful and forward-looking of all angling groups in Scotland, perhaps in Britain. Their name is the United Clyde Angling Protective Association Ltd.

Population and industry had a lot to do with the formation of the Association. After the Industrial Revolution, shipbuilding, heavy engineering and mining activities followed in a clattering, tumultuous, booming spread from the city of Glasgow itself right across the industrial belt and south into Lanarkshire. The population exploded to such an extent that most people in Scotland lived and worked in this wide area from Glasgow to Edinburgh. It was inevitable that three powerful forces would collide. The first was the desire of miners, steelworkers and other workers to get to the fresh air and beauty of the pastoral and moorland countryside in upper Lanarkshire,

particularly at weekends. The second force was industry with the local authorities of the towns doing little, or nothing, to protect the Clyde from pollution. The third was the rapidly increasing interest in fishing, particularly amongst the miners who craved the fresh air of the countryside, to say nothing of the opportunity to supplement their meagre food supplies with good trout.

In the face of these forces, two men in 1887 set themselves the objective of making the top part of the Clyde, that is, the part in Lanarkshire well clear of industry, into a first-class trouting water. The first man was William Robertson from Glasgow, whose father was a well known and enthusiastic Border angler. The second was the postmaster in the village of Abington whose name was Matthew McKendrick. They inspired others to join them, including the riparian owners who shared their aims.

In 1892 they built their own hatchery just outside Abington and this was supervised by

Holy Loch on the Clyde

several generations of McKendricks; the best known was another Matthew who served the association for twenty-five years. When he died in 1926 at the age of seventy-seven, his angling friends came to the funeral from all over the west of Scotland. Shortly afterwards, they erected a monument to his memory which can be seen today on the west bank of the Clyde, a mile north of Abington. The inscription reads, 'Fish fair and free, but spare the wee anes.'

By 1898, word had spread about the success of the enterprise and a meeting was held in Motherwell, the result of which was that the group became a branch of the United Clyde Angling Protective Association Ltd. Year by year all kinds of progress was made. A hundred thousand trout per year were released into the river; the pike population was controlled by gifts of prizes for each one caught; pollution in many tributaries was at least stemmed. Then in 1936, they found a disused curling pond in Abington and converted it into a larger and better stocking area. By the end of the Second World War, there were over a thousand members and it was not until 1974 that the price of an annual permit rose to £1. All the money was returned year after year for the purchase of fish stock and for the expenses of running the hatcheries.

The fight against pollution, even in those quiet, arcadian upper reaches of the river, required more than money to win it. It was a long, drawn-out conflict of interests, involving persuasion, influence, argument and dedication by lovers of the Clyde.

In 1869, no salmon had been seen in the Clyde since 1860 and, not surprisingly, evidence was given to the Rivers Pollution Commission that the once pure water was now nothing less than an open sewer. Downstream in Glasgow, the stench from the river even forced trippers to travel to the coastal resorts by train rather than 'doon the water' by paddle steamer.

The growth of industry around the towns of Motherwell, Wishaw and Hamilton kept pace with that around Glasgow itself and little was being done to stem the flow of poisonous wastes being pumped into the river. Some rather weak and ineffective laws were passed during those years, but it was not until 1903 that five cases against offenders were success-fully raised in the courts. This was a break-through, particularly as one of the offenders was the Burgh of Motherwell itself. By this time, a more enlightened view was being taken by the local town authorities and seven large burghs in Lanarkshire constructed sewage treatment plants.

When the Clyde River Purification Board was established in 1956, the Clyde anglers, through their association, had one member represented. The setting up of river boards throughout Scotland in 1951 was not welcomed by local authorities, simply because in certain areas they were the worst polluters. Nevertheless, these boards are now a fact of life and it must be said that the Clyde Board has proved its worth in the most dramatic terms possible. Salmon are now returning to the Clyde in considerable numbers around Glasgow.

These salmon have posed many problems, in which the Association has been very vocal and involved. The result of these years of contro-versy has resulted in the salmon lease for the Clyde above Bothwell being entrusted to the Association. This is a well-founded trust in a body of angling people who, for a hundred years on their own initiative, have done so much to protect and further the interests of anglers on the river. To say the least, it will ensure that the interests of salmon fishing on this famous river will be handled with the same unselfish dedication as it has been for trout fishing through all those years of frustration and problems.

In those parts of the river where no associ-ation has any claim, the Upper Clyde people have strong representation on the Clyde Fisheries Management Trust, which was set up to manage the unclaimed parts. It is not outside the scope of imagination to visualise the day when this enterprising group of people may be entrusted with almost the entire river and all its fishings.

Mayfly time on the Elvan

There was a time when I knew more about the Elvan and its trout than most people. The

The 'Half Moon' pool on the Clyde.

reason was simple. For twelve years my wife and I owned a little 200-year-old cottage at Elvanfoot, right on the river bank where the Elvan meets the Clyde, a mile or so from the source of the big river.

The cottage is still there. It was once the village smithy, then its schoolhouse, and over-looked the Clyde, just where Elvan Water sweeps down to form one of the most glorious pools for trout fishing I have ever known. Looking over the little footbridge, I have seen some enormous trout lying nonchalantly behind the rocks, their tails gently swaying in the current as they slowly and easily fed on the insects floating downstream.

In all those twelve years I never caught one of those monsters, even at night, but I did have more than my share of three-quarter-pounders, fishing both upstream dry fly and downstream wet.

It took me a long time to open a flirtation with Elvan Water. And like most successful flirtations that come to anything, I had to be introduced. The man who did this was called Eric Carpenter, an Edinburgh schoolmaster, who turned up one glowing Saturday morning in early summer and set up his rod and line outside our cottage.

'You have a fine morning for it,' I said, leaning against the edge of our door.

He looked up. 'How's the Elvan been doing lately?'

'I wouldn't know. I never fish it.'

'You're kidding! At *this* time of the year? The Mayfly season?' He stared at me.

I smiled foolishly. 'I've never fished Mayfly.' Then I tried to save face. 'They tell me they're only smallish fish in the Elvan, anyway,'

'Is that right? He smiled. 'Well, we'll see.'

It was the late afternoon when he knocked at our door.

'Hello.' I said, 'How did you do?'

He grinned and opened his wicker creel. Inside were a dozen good-size trout, from half-pounders up to two beauties each over a pound.

It taught me two lessons about small tributaries running into a main river. The first is never to judge the fishing potential by the size of the stream; the second is how to fish with the Mayfly during its brief season. Something else, however, came out of that short meeting with the schoolteacher who, incidentally, was also a very good angling teacher. He returned the following Saturday and we went up the Elvan together while he showed me the way to stalk the trout. He showed me how to dry fly upstream in a smallish stream and keep out of the skyline. I got three lovely trout in an afternoon.

If you ask anyone, even a Glaswegian, to tell you where the Clyde begins, they will say without hesitation. 'Same place as the Tweed.' Others will tell you a different tale. And usually all will be wrong.

When we first bought our cottage at Elvanfoot those many years ago, I really thought that that was the source of the Clyde — right outside our front door where Elvan Water meets the main river. And, of course, I was wrong.

As the early savants have always said, the Clyde begins in the same hills as the Tweed — the Lowther Hills — but on the *other* side altogether from the Tweed. Neil Munroe, the famous novelist, wrote a book in 1907 called *The Clyde* and in it he referred to the many arguments that had been going on for years about the source of the world-famous river. He settled for the Little Clyde Burn and, for my part, I see no reason to differ. Some people still say it is the Daer Water, some say the Powtrail Burn.

T. C. F. Brotchie, another author who followed Neil Munro in 1914 with his book *Glasgow Rivers and Streams*, told of a meeting he had with a local man who said that before the Caledonian Railway opened its line through the area in 1840, there was a burn called the Little Clyde which flowed west and joined the Daer Water at Elvanfoot. Its course was diverted by the railway engineers when the line was being built and it now flows south and joins the Elvan.

Many years later, Jack House, famous for his books about Glasgow, told of walking the whole length of the river in 1941 and ending up at the source of the Daer Water. Indignant natives of Lanarkshire wrote letters to the editor of his newspaper saying that he was completely wrong. And the dissension between one view and another is still going on to this day.

No matter where the source of the Clyde really is, be assured that these headwaters are a veritable paradise for the trout angler who likes lonely moorland country and who has the patience and time to bend his knees, keep out of the skyline and cast delicately upstream with a good eye. As he fishes, he will be surrounded by the ghosts of many famous and talented people who lived in the area for long and short periods. Wilson Barrett, the celebrated actor, lived at Watermeetings House for a while and, appropriate to his most famous play *The Sign of the Cross*, he is commemorated by a stained glass window in Elvanfoot church. John Masefield also stayed and wrote his poetry at Watermeetings. Nearby is the farm of Nunnerie where the Scottish poet Bessie J. B. MacArthur lived for some years. Far up in the hills, where the Elvan Water really has its source, is the village of Leadhills, where gold was first mined by the Romans to send to their mint near Edinburgh, and whose camp remains are nearby and where Dorothy and William Wordsworth and Coleridge stayed in 1803. They were not very impressed with the service they received at the inn in the village. From my experience the service at this Leadhills inn is now of the very best.

To get back to the Mayfly on the Elvan. The Mayfly is a large insect which lives in the gravel of clean streams in the nymph stage. It stays there for about two years then, when the temperature of the water is suitable, ascends to the surface and is carried by the current to emerge as a grown insect which flies into the air. After mating the female returns to the water to lay eggs. Then both male and female lie on the surface as spent flies and, of course, are at the mercy of the trout.

The whole life cycle, from nymph to spent insect, takes twenty-four hours, then the cycle begins all over again from the eggs that are laid. All this happens from the middle of May to the middle of June approximately, but the real feeding frenzy usually lasts only two weeks. During this time the fish are snatching at the Mayflies in all the stages of their life. At this time it is very difficult to tempt the trout on the Elvan with any other kind of fly; their minds seem bent on one insect only.

Living as we did next door to this excellent little stream, it was relatively easy for me to fish early in the morning or late into the evening in summer. And it was those early morning adventures going up the Elvan during the Mayfly hatch that were the most thrilling for me. The size and ferocity of these trout, which otherwise I would never have dreamed existed in such a small tributary, always amazed me.

Elvan Water, like the other tributaries of the Clyde in its upper reaches, is under the control of the United Clyde Angling Protective Association Ltd which has been managing these waters since 1887 under one kind of authority or another. This association is one of the oldest in the country and permits for their fisheries are issued from tacklists in the various towns and villages, as well as from hotels in Lanarkshire.

Poachers in the fog (Machrie)

When I was a boy, I camped in the summertime with two chums on the island of Arran, which lies off the Ayrshire coast. We pitched our tent in a delightful meadow, just up from the shore beyond the village of Lochranza. It was called Catacol Bay. One afternoon we hiked into the hills and, after climbing for an hour, we met a man with his two sons who were also camping. We stayed with them and shared a meal by their fire.

I remember this so well because the man, a schoolteacher, was a brilliant talker and held our attention of over an hour while he explained why Arran had vegetation and animal life and mountainous contours which were quite different from those just across the water in Ayrshire. He said that the diagonal line so clearly seen on a map of Scotland dividing the Highlands from the Lowlands (that is the one

you see on a map following the Caledonian Canal from Inverness down to Fort William) continued right under the sea to emerge in a volcanic peak which was the island of Arran. This, he explained, was why Arran had the same flora and fauna as was found farther north in the Highlands, whereas just a few miles across in Ayrshire the general scenery and geography were quite different.

We listened to all this open-mouthed and I never forgot that schoolteacher, whether he was right or wrong. What I do know is that Arran is a splendid Highland island and it has one predominant little river well worth fishing called the Machrie Water. It rises in the mountains in Ben Nois and only a few miles of it are fishable. Indeed you can see the peat-dark flats and deep rocky pools if you stop your car on the main road round the island and walk upstream along the bank.

I did this last year while on Arran with my wife visiting friends. I did not intend fishing. Indeed, I doubted if I could get a permit anyway because the Estate Office which manages the Machrie is at Killiechassie in Aberfeldy in Perthshire, and I knew that they let the fishings out on a weekly basis booked as early as January.

As luck would have it, I met the gamekeeper, and as he knew me by my weekly talks on the BBC, we discussed the river. As I expected, he said that the water just offshore was poached a great deal. He recalled autumn fogs that settled right down the river and out into the estuary. Then, when the fog lifted, half a dozen small craft with nets pulling in salmon and sea trout were in full view as if the curtains on a stage were raised and the scene lit up.

'Can't anyone stop the poachers?' I asked.

'Yes,' he said, 'the fisheries control vessel, but that's stationed miles across the firth at Helensburgh. It would take them hours to get over here, and by that time the poachers are gone.'

For all the deprivation caused by these offshore poachers, the Machrie is quite a favourable little river for salmon and sea trout. It has deep rocky pools and gushing streams in its lower few miles and rises and falls very quickly. During periods of plenty of water, there is some excellent sea trout fishing in various places where the fish are resting — Duke's Pool, Morton's Pool, Lady Mary Pool,

Duchess Pool, Sharps' Pool and Shepherds' Pool.

While the Machrie does not offer a bonanza for the sea trout angler (less than a hundred sea trout is the yearly average) it is a beautiful water in a beautiful Scottish island.

The wee river at Holy Loch (Echaig)

I have had two experiences of the Echaig river. This is a fine little water which runs from Loch Eck into Holy Loch. It is only four-and-a-half miles long from where it leaves the loch until it reaches the Firth of Clyde.

The first time I saw it, or even heard of it, was when I bought a residential caravan for weekends for my family and me at the south end of Loch Eck, indeed just where the river starts. We enjoyed those weekends. I bought a little boat, sailed it on the loch and caught a few brown trout and sea trout.

The river, which babbled its way behind our caravan and just over the fence, fascinated me. So I enquired about fishing from the owners of the caravan site, and was assured it was all right for me to fish it. So I did. I would like to say that it was teeming with trout and sea trout and that I filled a basket. It would be quite untrue. I caught two sea trout each under a pound and that was that.

There was no doubt it was a spate river. When Loch Eck was up in height, then the river was big and I am sure that would be the time to get the fish. I also discovered something else, I had no right to fish it. The fishing rights at that time were in some dispute, the mouth was

Waiting for the fish to rise.

Glendaruel on the Cowal Peninsula through which the Echaig runs.

being netted, and some of the locals to whom I spoke in the pub down at Sandbank obviously did not want to talk about who owned what. So I dropped the subject in the face of this silence; a situation not unfamiliar in certain fishing areas in Scotland. I simply did not fish the water again in order to avoid getting into trouble.

That was many years ago, and I now know that this little sea trout river has had its ownership properly established and that it is now well managed and controlled, partly on a time-share basis and partly being let. I know this because a friend of mine, a Swiss doctor, with his son fished it for a week in July and caught virtually nothing. I met him at the airport on his way home.

'That's a mystery,' I said. 'That river has always been famous for its sea trout'.

'I can well believe it.'

'What happened?'

'Nothing.'

'Did you see any fish?'

'Plenty.' He sighed and looked at his son. 'And they were saying "goodbye". Not resting at all. Straight up through to Lock Eck as fast as torpedoes.'

I then asked him where he was fishing, when and with what tackle. Regarding the pools, neither he nor his son could hardly go far wrong in such a short river, so there was little doubt that, with their wide experience of sea trout, they were in the right places. And as far as I could tell, the flies they were using were excellent for sea trout on that water — Teal and Silver, Brown Turkey, Invictor, Peter Ross. The nylon casts, the lines, the rods — I could find nothing out-of-the-way.

'When were you fishing?'

'Daytime.'

'Ah-ha!'

I felt and still feel I had the answer to their problem of a blank week. Certainly there had been no rain, and when that happens for a whole week on the Echaig, an angler's activities are virtually condensed to a few hours at sunset and beyond. Naturally, neither the good doctor nor his son, would accept that catching sea trout on this Argyllshire river could only be achieved at night. But, as we said goodbye, I could tell by the doubtful look in their eyes, that they really felt I was right.

The Echaig, particularly regarding its fishing rights, has had a checkered history. In his book *The Salmon Rivers of Scotland* published in 1909, W. L. Calderwood says,

> 'In the first three years of the present proprietors' time the netting was let to a tacksman in Dunoon and in this period, I have been informed, he secured 33,000 sea trout.'

Eleven thousand sea trout a year as a net catch from a river four-and-a-half miles long is some haul!

Loch Eck is probably the narrowest loch in Scotland, so narrow in fact that it might well be a continuation of the River Cur which empties into it and an extension of the Echaig six miles down. It is, however, a deep loch, average depth 139 feet, and it holds salmon, sea trout and brown trout as well as fish of the Ice Age — Powan and Char.

In spite of my Swiss friends' disappointing experience on the Echaig, there are some big sea trout to be caught on the river. In 1977 a boy angler caught one weighing 15 lb, and fish up to 20 lb have been taken in the nets at the mouth.

These big fish were certainly never there in the daytime when my Swiss friend and his son fished the river for a full week!

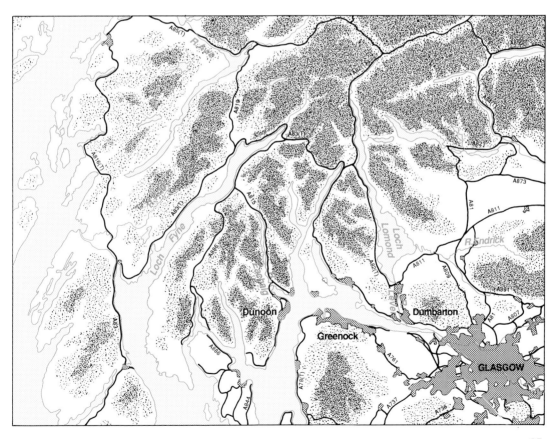

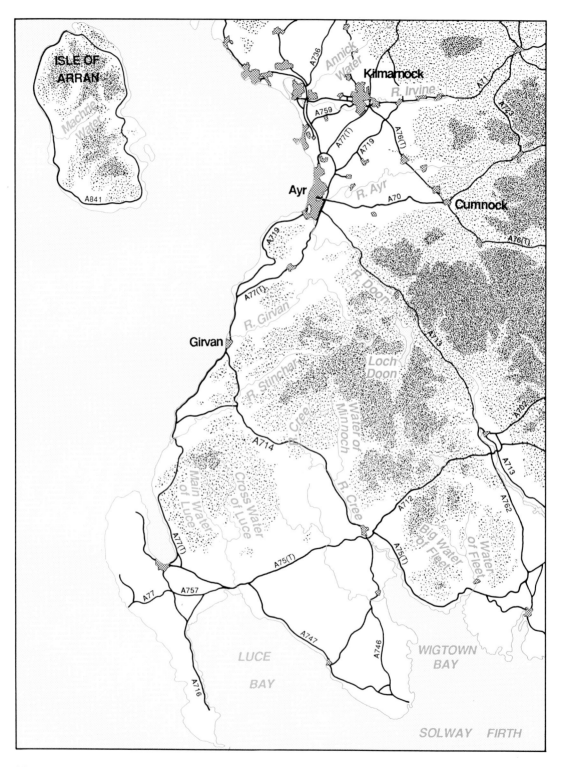

Ayrshire

The rivers

Ayr · Girvan · Doon · Stinchar · Irvine · Annick

Get-up-and-go Girvan

I had a poor impression of the Girvan, long before I even saw this Ayrshire river. It happened this way.

For many years I have broadcast about angling every Saturday morning on BBC Radio Scotland, and if there was to be a telephone discussion with some expert on the subject, I always liked to prepare myself and the other person in advance. On this particular week I contacted a well-known and somewhat aristocratic riparian owner whose water was near the Girvan and I prepared both of us for the discussion on the Saturday.

'So you have the idea, sir — nothing negative or gloomy?' I said.

'Absolutely.'

'I'll ask you about the present state of the fishing and you tell me all the good things — numbers of fish caught, who caught them and what flies were used. All right?'

'Splendid.'

'Cheerful and uplifting?'

'Rely on me.'

Saturday morning came. I assured the producer that Mr Riparian Owner had a good voice and that we would be discussing the pleasant and agreeable aspects of fishing on the rivers in Ayrshire and his river in particular. (I knew how the producer felt about 'attitudes' to a subject.) He promised to switch him through to me on the telephone so that I could conduct the interview in the studio 'live'.

The broadcast was a disaster. Unknown to me, this particular gentleman had been harbouring a long term grudge against the National Coal Board and others who, without doubt, had been polluting the headwaters of rivers in Ayrshire for years, particularly the Girvan. And now that he was on the air, contrary to our agreement, he was determined to voice his grievances long and loud.

'But —,' I tried to interrupt his full flight.

'But nothing. I want people to know what's happening to our rivers in this part of Scotland.'

'May I —?'

'No, you may not. Listen to me . . .' And on and on he went until the furious producer literally 'pulled the plug' on him.

Quite apart from the scorching I endured from the producer at the end of that broadcast, any mention of the River Girvan from then on sent shivers down my back. If the Coal Board had polluted its waters, who would want to fish it?

How wrong I was to let an opinion like that condition my view of a splendid little river! It was only last year that I visited the water and talked to a few anglers — and there were many that Saturday evening. I was returning with a friend from a day on the Stinchar at Barr and we took the B7023 back road on our way north. This is how I came upon the Water of Girvan and the people fishing it.

The river is only twenty-three miles long at its fishable part and it is easy to see how careless practices could pollute such a fine stream.

Towards the end of 1977, the National Coal Board stopped operating Dalquhanan Colliery near Dailly. The shaft was sealed off and pumping operations ceased. The Board were warned by officials from the Clyde River Purification Board that the water level in the shaft would rise and pit water containing harmful metal chemicals would emerge within two years.

99

This is exactly what happened. In October 1979 half a million gallons of water contaminated with iron and aluminium went into the River Girvan every day by way of a small tributary. The result was the massacre of thousands of fish and the virtual destruction of all angling sport along six miles of the lower river. There was a court action, of course, and in July 1980 the NCB was found guilty. They appealed but lost the case. The punishment? A fine of £750.

Today, pollution has stopped and migrating fish are returning to the Girvan. And with the support of Girvan District Salmon Fishery Board, local angling clubs have set up a small hatchery for the purpose of restocking some of the tributaries. Together with an increasing stock of brown trout, the water is now very popular and on the particular Saturday I walked along its banks, there was one angler every ten or twenty yards.

In the lower reaches of the river, from Crosshill down to the estuary, the sea trout fishing is first class, particularly in the deep evening or at night. Nearer the sea, the light facing west is very good and the summer angler is rarely fishing 'blind'.

In a way, I was especially pleased to see so many anglers fishing the Girvan that autumn Saturday evening. Some of them were miners from the landward colliery areas around Dalmellington and it was obvious that there were entire clubs on the water. Someone once said to me in another connection, 'If you see a lot of flies around a honeypot, don't be put off.' You can be sure of one thing — there is a lot of honey! And this was my thought when seeing those groups of anglers on a water that generations of colliery owners, by neglect, had almost killed as a fishing river time and time again.

Long before the pollution dispute in 1979, the Girvan suffered an even worse disaster. In February 1902 a large coal pit had eighteen months previously taken fire. It was flooded and shut down. Then the owners reopened it and began pumping out the water which was carried into a burn near Dailly. The burn turned a bright orange colour and when water from the burn entered the Girvan eight-and-a-half miles from the mouth, every fish from this point to the sea died. The water in the main river was like pea soup. The pumping went on month after month and as all this happened before the organisation of river purification boards, no one stopped the practice until the whole river became fishless.

Like many anglers, I am rarely delighted to see a heavy population of others on 'my' part of the water, especially when seeking some privacy, but I was pleased that Saturday evening to witness the rebirth of a fine little angling river, to see it reach maturity and give pleasure to so many anglers after almost a century of being brought to death's door twice by poisoning.

On reflection, perhaps I should have been more sympathetic about the views of that riparian owner during my broadcast interview with him. Whatever he was trying to say must have done some good.

'Ye Banks and Braes O'Bonnie Doon'

Although I know that Scotland's national bard Robert Burns fished the river Nith during the time he farmed in Dumfries, I can find no evidence that he ever fished the river, which flowed past the cottage of his birth and where he spent his young life, at Alloway two miles from Ayr. But I would be surprised if he had not wielded a fishing rod over the river Doon by the old bridge of Alloway.

After the last war pollution from the collieries around Dalmellington almost made the river ruinous for anglers. Strong protests, some court actions and, better still, a lot of co-operation from the National Coal Board over the years have resulted in purer water, an increasing fish population and better angling for all of the Ayrshire rivers like the Girvan, the Ayr and the Stinchar. Today the Doon has almost returned to its former state as a salmon, sea trout and brown trout river of some distinction in Scotland. (Let no one forget that Mr J. Burn caught a brown trout of 13 lb on the Doon in 1965.)

A view across the bay to the town of Ayr.

The river rises in a beautiful area of moorland, the part of South Ayrshire that meets Kircudbrightshire, which is too often neglected by tourists who seem obsessed in their drive up from the south with the Trossachs, the Highlands, Edinburgh and Royal Deeside. The headwaters of the river come from Loch Enoch, 1,700 feet above sea level, and they flow into the head of Loch Doon which is part of a complex hydro electric scheme, one of the first in Scotland. There is a dam forty-four feet high at the foot of the loch and below this the river roars down through a gorge into Ness Glen. At one time a channel was made in the gorge to facilitate the passage of salmon up into the loch. Now, since the dam was built, there is a very interesting circular fish ladder inside a tower which does the same job and salmon ascend through it in a spiral fashion to get to the loch.

From the loch, the river runs through Dalmellington for a mile or so to Bogton Loch, then it has a run of sixteen miles until it reaches the sea at Burns' birthplace, Brig o' Doon, in Alloway. This stretch of the river is particularly pastoral in its beauty, as is the rest of the countryside in the farmlands of South Ayrshire.

Loch Doon, from which flows the river proper, is four miles long and is partly in Kirkcudbrightshire but mainly in Ayrshire. It is 680 feet above sea level and is studded with five groups of islands. Among them is Castle Island, on which stand the remains of a very old tower, called Baliol's Castle. It is supposed to be the place where King Alpin of Dalriada died in 741. And a sister of Robert the Bruce is said to have lived there when she became the wife of Seaton, the local laird.

For an angler, the Doon is now a river that is improving every year. A trout angler fishing with a size 10 Stoat's Tail tube fly must not be too surprised if he has the hair-raising experience of a salmon going for it — and this is sometimes the case on this river. Although brown trout fishing is fairly steady all spring and summer, July and August are the best months for small sea trout and finnock, even though they are fastidious and unpredictable about the flies they prefer — one day one thing, another day something else.

Up where the trout lies dreaming (Stinchar)

People who want to catch fish first and foremost, really have no business behind a fishing rod. They are like art connoisseurs who want the canvas and the oils and the paint instead of the painting.

I feel somebody should say this because many of us are a bit tired of answering silly questions when we return from a fishing trip, about how many fish we caught, or what size they were or why on earth we travelled so far and spent so much time catching nothing. In a way, most of us are really deceivers, pretending to be determined experts, whereas really we just want to be up where the trout lies dreaming by a mountain stream and on the edge of the world. The whole business of getting our gear ready, sorting out flies with infinite care and packing sandwiches, is part of the rigmarole for getting to the sweeping heathered hills and the sun-dappled trout pools. I do not suppose for one minute that we would drive a hundred miles over hill and dale, tramp over gorse and grass just to sit on a rock and drink coffee and admire the riverside. People who love the mountains and the sky and the trees and the flowing river must have some reason for going there. Ours is fishing.

We like to catch fish. But that is not the real reason for the trip. It is the dawn start and the thrill of anticipation, the talk and the palaver

Fishing for sunset sea trout on the Stinchar

and just being somewhere that looks the way it is. It is the fishing — not the fish.

I mention these thoughts with many rivers in mind, particularly a relatively small one in the south of Ayrshire called the Stinchar.

One August day when you motor down the A77 from Ayr, passing Turnberry and the famous hotel and golf course, through the little seaside town of Girvan, following the Ayrshire coast all the way, look over at the sugar loaf of Ailsa Craig standing out of the ocean, the island from which most of the world's curling stones came, made from its hard granite rock. Then carry on down past Lendalfoot on the edge of Ballantrae Bay (wondering why your car has to get into a lower gear to go *downhill* at the phenomenon of the Electric Brae) and stop at the Ballantrae bridge and look over at the estuary of the river. Keep looking and you will see on the smooth surface of the water the widening rings and the occasional plops and splashes of fish. What you are looking at is the mouth of one of Ayrshire's finest trout and sea trout rivers, the Stinchar.

This river starts in one of the most unheralded and beautiful areas of the Scottish Lowlands. Carrick and Galloway have tracts of ancient forests, rolling hills and sparse populations. Glentrool Forest, Penninghame Forest and Kirroughtree Forest overlook a vast, wild, countryside of fells, moors and glens that deserve many more tourists and visitors than those who simply motor through on their way north to what they think is the real Scotland. The Stinchar has its source just north of this area in South Ayrshire, on the western slope of the Doon watershed, and flows twenty-seven miles to the Atlantic at Ballantrae, where you will see restless fish waiting for the freshwater coming down river from the hills.

The Stinchar rises close to the source of the Girvan and it flows west. Throughout its course it has a gravelly bed and alternating pools and streams which are a delight to see and fish. It is a spate river, however, and its character can change rapidly from a gently-babbling stream to a yellow torrent that thrashes its way down the hills.

The river has two tributaries, the Tig and the Duisk, both of which enter the river from the south. The Tig is the smaller burn with a length of eight miles and joins the Stinchar only two-and-a-half miles from the mouth. The Tig is

therefore the spawning target for many sea trout, since they do not like to be too far away from salt water. The Duisk is the larger tributary and it rises from some small burns close to the headwaters of the Bladenach. It flows about ten miles to the Stinchar at Pinwherry.

Permits to fish the Stinchar are not widely publicised. There are many riparian owners, but tickets can be purchased at various places, depending on the value of individual areas, from the Barr Angling Club or from the hotel at Barr. At Colmonell, the local guest house can get tickets, or they can be obtained from the head gamekeeper in the village. The four major owners of fishings are the estates of Dalreoch, Bardrocher, Knockdolian and Stair and hopeful applications can be made to them.

If we were taken to a reservoir bank beside a steelworks and it was stiff with large trout, we would run a mile in the opposite direction. Those of us who fish for trout do not want big ones that badly. Our fishing place has to look right and the surroundings have to be right before we feel we are angling. Anything else strikes us as fishmongering.

The Stinchar, in my opinion, is the embodiment of everything a trout or sea trout angler would want.

A river in the lace-making country (Irvine)

There was a time when every river in Scotland contained migrating fish and most of them had resident brown trout as well. It is difficult to imagine now how nearly all of them in the central belt, right out to the east and west coasts, were decimated. This wholesale fish genocide was caused by a variety of ingredients — booming mills, mines and factories, tremendous rises in population, indifferent sewage disposal policies by the towns and cities, and an ever-increasing demand for water abstraction. Within a matter of fifty years the rivers were barren of fish life.

Then man — the real cause of all this — awoke slowly and various fisheries acts and prevention of pollution laws were passed piece by piece.

It is a miracle that many of these rivers survived as fishing waters. But they did. One of them in North Ayrshire is called the Irvine. In the eighteenth and nineteenth centuries the lower reaches were extensively dammed to provide water power for the many textile, mainly lace, mills. Some of the dams are still there but although the lack of water flow can restrict the methods of fishing, the Dreghorn Angling Club manages the water very well. Their fishings start at Lave Saw Mill and in the flats from here down to Daybridge Dam the water is rather featureless. Nevertheless, it is well stocked with brown trout which rise freely in late spring and on summer evenings.

Farther downstream the river charges as far as Holmsford Bridge and between the alternating streams and flats the fishing is very pleasant.

The Dreghorn Angling Club was first started in 1925 and looks after the fishing on two rivers in this area, the Irvine and the Annick. They do this very well. Although salmon and sea trout run the rivers, the best and most dependable fishing is for brown trout. On the Irvine the bottom is usually very muddy, so wellington boots not waders are advisable; the fishing from the bank is comfortable and easy.

The other river, Annick Water, is a pleasant little trout stream. The water is very clear, so fine tackle with small flies are best and dry-fly fishing is well advised. This stream is a tributary of the Irvine.

The main river runs through an area that was once very prosperous and, indeed, had a world-wide reputation for its lace-making. It runs from Darvel and Newmilns to Galston and Kilmarnock. It is a classic small lowland river and anglers should be grateful to the association of clubs, which have grown in competence and enthusiasm since the 1920s.

The largest brown trout caught recently on the Irvine was one of 5¼ lb and sea trout between 8 and 10 lb have been known although they are normally caught weighing 2-4 lb. Although there is no limit on the numbers of salmon or sea trout which may be caught, there is a limit of six brown trout per rod.

Who needs salmon? (Ayr)

Many rivers in the Highlands, even the small ones, are endowed with good luck. They are well away from the pollution of industry. They have migrating fish coming up them at various times of the year and, most importantly, they are sufficiently remote to discourage most poachers most of the time. As a further deterrent to fish-thieves, those that are important angling rivers, like the Oykel, the Helmsdale and the Naver, are well managed.

If some owners of lesser-known waters had the opportunity to improve the quality and increase the catch of salmon and sea trout by means of some capital outlay, I believe they would not hesitate. As evidence of this, just consider what Thurso Fisheries Limited have achieved on their river over many years to improve the fishing; they have managed to control the source-water at Loch More and have created dams to encourage more salmon upstream.

When pollution and poachers are not present, almost anything is possible in Highland rivers.

It is a different story altogether in the Lowlands. From the east to the west coast of Scotland, south of Stirling and within striking distance of what were the industrial centres of Glasgow and Edinburgh, angling clubs, protection associations and fishing owners are often at their wits' end defending their waters against pillagers and polluters. This is particularly true of waters which have salmon and sea trout in them. Sometimes they win, sometimes they lose. A lot depends on how sparsely populated, or otherwise, is the county through which the river flows. The struggle to protect some of the rivers near industrial areas has been given up and those waters are almost barren. Others, like the Nith, which flows from the once huge coal-mining areas of New Cumnock, Kirkconnel and Sanquhar down past Thornhill and Dumfries to empty into the Solway Firth, have not only survived but are success stories of good organisation and co-operation.

Now that heavy industry and coal mining is in decline in many parts of Scotland, some of the lowland rivers are presenting their fishery owners and angling clubs with a dilemma. With the decrease in pollution and the activities of the river purification boards, some rivers are stirring out of their long sleep and are increasingly welcoming the return of salmon and sea trout, to say nothing of providing a healthier home for the resident brown trout. This is true in Ayrshire and particularly on the River Ayr.

This fine river is the largest in Ayrshire. It is thirty-nine miles long and, considering its route from the one-time busy industrial area of north Ayrshire down to the town of Ayr itself where it empties into the harbour of that busy, busy town, it really is a miracle that migrating fish have struggled through its hazards for so many years since the Industrial Revolution. That it is still a reasonably good fishing river at all is due in no small measure to the efforts of the angling clubs at Ayr, Ladykirk, Annbank, Mauchline, Catrine, Sorn and Muirkirk and the local river purification board.

The dilemma the owners, lessees and managers face is a simple one. Should they help to restore the river for salmon and sea trout or should they leave things as they are and let nature have her way?

As far as salmon are concerned, man and his greed are part of 'natures' way when there is prospect of big runs of fish in thirty-nine miles of largely unprotected water. The prospect of easy money and low risk of prosecution are the poachers' main motivation and this has been evident for years on many of Ayrshire's rivers. Now that much of the Ayr has been cleaned up, and the salmon and sea trout and brown trout are still there in goodly numbers, should those interested in the river do more to bring back more migrating fish? Should they remove weirs or cauls to make it easier for the fish to pass? If so, why? More salmon means, as well as better angling, more poaching. And more poaching means more river-watchers which means, one way or another, more expense.

As it flows presently, the Ayr is a very pleasant river. It reaches the sea about a mile north of the Doon. It is a pastoral kind of river running through fertile country and there are good streams with gravel beds in the lower reaches that give excellent sport for trout and, in summer, for sea trout. Tarholm and Auchincruive are the best places for trouting with dry fly, and English anglers used to the gentle, weedy waters of southern chalk streams will feel at home on this part of the river.

In a way, the dilemma of the Ayr is not unlike that of the Clyde. Now that migrating fish have returned to the Clyde after a hundred years because of purer water, should they be encouraged to surmount the steep Falls of the Clyde at New Lanark by constructing a fish ladder as they have done at Pitlochry? There are some trout anglers along the 26 miles of water above the Falls who say 'no'. They fear that once salmon are established in 'their' upper river they may even lose their trouting; the pressure for salmon fishing being so strong and the potential for poaching being what it is.

They have a case. Brown trout do not attract poachers to the same extent and many regular anglers on the Ayr want their river to remain as it is — a very good trouting water.

Spring afternoon on an Ayrshire river.

Loch Lubnaig, headwater of many east-central streams.

Edinburgh and the Borders

The rivers

Tweed · Teviot · Whiteadder · Yarrow · Water of Leith ·
Esk · Almond · Tyne

The River Tweed at Innerleithen.

Tweed — more than a river

If Scotland had no other river worth fishing but still had most of the Tweed, the country would still be world famous for the quality of its sports angling. The Tweed is more than a 100-mile river, it is a water catchment area draining almost 1,700 square miles. Its many tributaries and small streams have been described as an entire paradise by fishermen over the last 200 years. Its waters are teeming with salmon, trout and other fish, all rolling, gliding, ripping and roaring through such a variety of countryside bordering England and giving pleasure to countless generations of anglers.

Among the hundreds of books about angling written by famous authors whose names have been legends since 1800, there are some which devote almost half their pages to the Tweed before condescending to describe other waters in Scotland. Some authors wrote general guides about Scottish fishing waters yet devoted the entire book to the River Tweed and its tributaries. In some of the early literature on the sport it is as if no other river or loch existed.

Of course, there were many reasons for this narrow-minded approach to angling in Scotland. Lack of adequate transport facilities was one; the Highlands, even in Sir Walter Scott's time, were still the Wild North, much of it unexplored, and the roads were impossible, to say nothing of the amenities. The Tweed was easily accessible from England and certainly from the blossoming city of Edinburgh, and in any case a goodly stretch of the river is in England. The natural pastoral beauty along Tweedside hardly needed Sir Walter Scott's novels to extol it. As it turned out, his romantic writing and his personal affinity to the splendour around Melrose and Kelso and Dryborough (he built a house and resided in Abbotsford) caused a virtual explosion of praises from anglers and tourists about the

river. When he was in his last days and was brought from abroad to die at Abbotsford, it is said that although Scott had been speechless and hardly moving for days, when the carriage came nearer his home, he rallied at once and began talking as if electrified as he gazed over the Tweed valley to the hills. He died shortly afterwards in the heart of his beloved Tweedside.

Apart from the beauty of its surroundings as it passes through the Scottish lowlands, as a fishing river the Tweed is better endowed than most others because of the tributes it receives from other streams in its majestic progress to the North Sea. Only the Tay can hope to match it for the number and extent of its feeder rivers and burns. Indeed, as far as comparisons go, in the songs of the Edinburgh Angling Club (1858) there is a verse from 'The Tweed':

> 'Let others discourse of the smooth-
> winding Tay
> Or tell of the charms of the swift-rolling
> Spey,

The famous Slap on the Tweed near Coldstream.

Of the Dee and the Don and the Forth
and the Clyde;
But I love fair Tweed as a bridegroom
his bride.'

The main tributaries of the Tweed start right up beyond Peebles with Biggar Water, then comes Lyne, Eddlestone and Manor Waters. Below the town comes Leithen Water, Quair, Yarrow, Ettrick, Gala, Leeder, and Borthwick Waters. Then there is the River Teviot, the largest of the tributaries, followed by Slitrig, Ale, Rule, Jed, Eden, Oxnam, Kale, Bowmount, Whiteadder, Blackadder and Leet Waters. There are College and Harthope Burns then the rivers Glen and Till.

It is interesting to observe the justifiable boast of the people of Peebles when they claim that the River Tweed in Peebles-shire, i.e. Tweedale, is the only place on the river where the general public has access at reasonable cost to fish for salmon, sea trout and brown trout. The Peebles-shire Trout Fishing Association control twenty-eight miles of the river plus four miles of Lyne Water. I can vouch for them as a well run association and they put all their profits back into the waters by stocking in March and October.

In comparison with the prices paid by anglers for the privilege of fishing on other parts of the Tweed, that claim by the Peebles association can be well understood. One thousand pounds for a week's salmon fishing on one of the more prolific stretches is about what it costs an enthusiast in spring or autumn. The prices come down, of course, for other beats at other times of the year but the pressure today by anglers for good beats is as strong as ever. It is not unknown, however, for an angler to fish a very expensive beat all week and catch nothing. When this happens, all sorts of reasons are put forward, ranging from poor water conditions in particular months to the activities of poachers who pay nothing and take hundreds of salmon from the water by every illegal means, from otter-boards to splash-nets and drift-nets in the estuary. Fingers have been pointed, however, at what some riparian owners see as the main culprits — the commercial netters who have been operating on the river quite legally for 300 years. Critics as eminent as Lord Home of the Hirsel, who owns large stretches of the river, and the Duke of Roxburgh, are on

record as saying that netting — albeit legal — has played its part in reducing salmon catches for anglers by over seventy-five per cent in the last twenty years.

At this stage there now enters the Atlantic Salmon Conservation Trust, with plenty of cash and a determination to see that the interests of tourism, a more profitable national activity than salmon netting, should take precedence and that the netters should simply be bought out. So they paid out over half a million pounds for fishing rights and thirty commercial net fisheries were closed down, from Coldstream in Scotland to the English estuary at Berwick-on-Tweed. The estimate is that 22,000 extra salmon will be moving upstream each season. In 1969 some 90,000 salmon were caught in nets. Fifteen years later the figure was less than 18,000. These figures speak for themselves and give good cause for the move by the Trust.

So much for salmon angling. What about trout and sea trout?

Stoddart in his book *The Angler's Companion to the Rivers and Lochs of Scotland*, published in 1853, tells of his friend John Wilson fishing the burns which flow into the Tweed catching twelve *dozen* trout in an afternoon, while Stoddart himself was catching them weighing 1 lb each below Thirlstane and saw one of 3 lb taken. On another occasion in the neighbourhood of Howman, he and Wilson caught 'thirty-six dozen' trout in a day. Without doubt, these days are over for trout anglers. Half a dozen fish of about three-quarters of a pound each would be a good day.

However, one aspect of trout fishing on the Tweed has not changed since Stoddart's day. Fishing for them on the main river is not as profitable or as enjoyable as on one of the many tributaries, at least in my opinion. The one exception to this is a mile or so downstream from Peebles. Of course, on the more expensive salmon beats, who can blame an angler for concentrating his entire week on the King of Fish and forgetting about the humble trout when he has paid so much for his fishing? The trouting on such feeding waters as the Gala and the Ettrick and the Yarrow, in the right conditions, is superb.

Although sea trout come up the Tweed in thousands to spawn, for some reason they are not so easy to catch by rod and line as on many other Scottish waters. When one is caught, however, it is often a monster. As far upstream as Peebles, Mr G. Levy caught one weighing 20 lb and it served as a British record. Although this is a fairly recent example, sea trout of well over 10 lb are quite frequently hooked.

The largest properly authenticated British sea trout, a monster of 28½ lb, was caught in the nets in the lower reaches of the Tweed in the autumn of 1988; its age was over five years and it had spawned only once. A fibreglass cast of this fish is on show at the Freshwater Fisheries Laboratory near Pitlochry.

As a result of tagging operations, it has been discovered that Tweed sea trout migrate from far distances. Many head down through the North Sea to the Norfolk and Suffolk coasts where they feed heavily on sand eels, sprats and small herring. Some even cross the North Sea and feed in areas off Holland and Denmark.

Apart from the excellence of the coarse fishing available around Kelso, the Tweed is indeed a paradise for game fishers. Although its salmon are world famed, trout fishing in the tributaries is beyond compare with any other comparable water in Britain. And for anglers who consider the fishing more important than the fish — the Tweed is more, much more, than a river.

Trouting Tweed

Some years ago when I was broadcasting about angling, there was a kind of off-the-air conversation that often took place with riparian owners, or river fishery managers, or local tacklists which usually began with me saying something like: —

'Well, that's very interesting, Mr Richards. I had no idea that you had such a big run of salmon in the spring on your river. I always imagined it was a "back end" river.'

'Really, it's both, Roderick. We have salmon galore in the spring *and* the autumn.'

'What about the trout fishing?'

Pause. No reply.

'I said "what about the trout?" '

'Well, now, I'd be obliged if you broadcast nothing about the trout fishing.'

'Oh? Why is that?'

'Well, to tell you the truth we're not too keen in encouraging too many trout anglers.'

'But your river has *marvellous* trout fishing — and tickets are available from the local associations.'

'Maybe so, but — well, some of these trout anglers are a bit of a problem.'

'Why is that?'

'Next time you're down this way, I'll tell you.'

It took me a long time to get to the bottom of this mystery. Trout anglers discouraged from fishing a salmon river? Why were they unwelcome when the local associations sold tickets?

The river warden on the Association stretch of the Tweed at Kelso gave me the answer as we stood on the river bank.

'Well, now, I'll tell you. I'm not meaning *all* trout fishers who come to Tweed are like this, but there *are* a few who cheat.'

'Oh? How?'

'You know that these new carbon fibre trout rods are so strong they'll hold a salmon all right. Well, sometimes when I ask to see a visiting angler's tackle and look at the flies he's using, what do I find? Big flies with leaded bodies. *He's* not fishing for trout — he's after salmon!'

'And that's why you don't encourage — ?'

'Right. We don't keep them *off* because we do allow trout fishing. But we *do* have to keep our eyes skinned for the leaded-fly brigade or the gobble-of-worms boys. That's why we don't say too much about our trout fishing.'

The advent of Protection Orders on most of Scotland's main salmon rivers has now curtailed much of this sort of cheating and since the Tweed's Order was taken out in 1980, the river is one of those to benefit by the law. And I am one of the many anglers who appreciate this because some of the best trout fishing I have ever enjoyed has been on the Tweed.

It would be misleading to classify as excellent for trout all the ninety-six miles of the Tweed from Manor Water three miles above Peebles to the wider stretches beyond Coldstream. The rate of flow of the river, the proximity of insect-bearing trees and foliage, the ease or difficulty of wading and casting at different

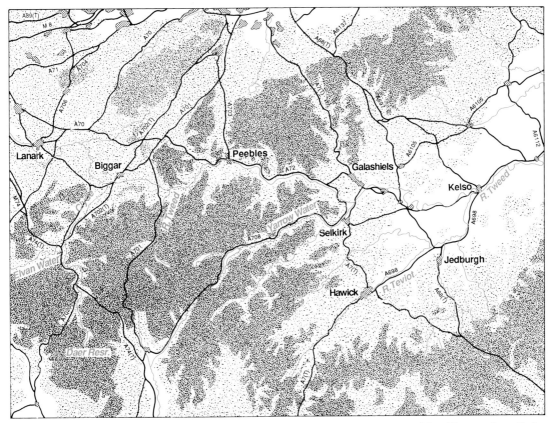

spots, the stocking programme, plus the prior claims of salmon anglers on certain private beats — all these negate any attempts at generalization. Indeed, any general description of Tweed trout will be of little use to an angler who just wants to know where to go, when to be there and roughly what it will cost him to fish for a day or a week. And that inevitably means personal preferences. To that extent I will give mine.

The most enjoyable trouting I have ever had on the river was on that series of glides three miles downstream from Peebles. This is a local association water and it is well managed. I can remember fishing with a friend, Bob McMillan, who was a dry-fly obsessionist; he fished no other way and kept preaching at me to give up my downstream 'wet' style in favour of 'reading' the water carefully, especially the rough, white water, and casting upstream with one silicon-treated fly. Of course, he was right (these dry fly people usually are). He caught more trout and bigger trout than me.

What he did was this. He used a little butterfly net to skim just above the water and take examples of the flies on which the fish were feeding. Then he carefully matched them from his book of artificial flies, sometimes repeating this process every hour or so and changing flies accordingly.

For my part, I doggedly fished downstream on a 'chuck-it-and-chance-it' basis with a team of three wet flies. My tail fly was always a Greenwell's Glory, thank goodness, and it certainly earned its worth. Not many people realise that this wonderful fly was made on the Tweed by a local Bowmount fly-tier called Jimmy Wright on the directions of a well-known angler called Canon Greenwell. The Canon was frustrated by his friend Mr Henderson who always caught more fish than he, so he took a box of natural flies, taken from the river, to Jimmy and got him to make exact imitations. The result was sensational and really made angling history. From then on, the Canon got the biggest catches and his fly

111

'Greenwell's Glory' has been the best all-rounder for trout ever since.

Fishing the stretch downstream from Peebles is relatively easy and inexpensive for the trout angler. The local fishing-tackle shop sells daily or weekly tickets for a few pounds, as well as giving excellent free advice to visitors.

Another favourite trouting stretch is at Kelso where the local angling association has eight miles of Tweed and Teviot, as well as water on the River Eden. There is no Sunday fishing and there are also restrictions on spinning. Ticket prices are very low, with concessions for pensioners and juniors, and permits are obtainable from local tacklists in the town.

In 1858 a book was published: *Guide Book to the Tweed and its Tributaries and other Streams — commanded by the North British Railway*. It contained these words:

> 'Never surely can Railways and Rivers run more lovingly together than the North British and its Branches and the Tweed and its Branches.'

The earliest recorded angling club was formed at Ellenford on the Whiteadder in 1828 but it was the advent of the railways in the 1850s that brought the Edinburgh lawyers and bankers and their clerks down to the waters of the Tweed and its tributaries. The road system today gives easy access to anglers from all over the Scottish lowlands and this is probably the reason why both trout and salmon fishing is so rigorously controlled and well managed. Incidentally, sea trout as a migrating fish, is like salmon fishing, mostly in private hands on the Tweed.

The river rises at Tweed's Well in the southern uplands of Scotland and flows through the majestic woods and lush parklands of Drumelzier and Dawick to Peebles, then on to Innerleithen and Walkerburn. The magnificent scenery of the Scottish lowland hills, the gentle pastoral lands and wooded grandeur described by Sir Walter Scott, and the richness of borderland history justifiably gives the Tweed an aura of paradise for anglers. The river rolls, tumbles and glides on into England via Coldstream to Berwick-on-Tweed, where it empties through a broad estuary into the North Sea.

Although most of the salmon fishing on the river is private, held either by riparian owners or leased by syndicates, the trout fishing at various spots is fairly easy to get and is also very inexpensive. St Boswell's and Melrose in Roxburghshire both have angling associations, the former with four-and-a-half miles and the latter with several excellent stretches. Both are open to visitors and the tickets are available at local tackle shops. The same applies in Galashiels, where the local association has twelve miles of the river as well as Gala Water, which is a very sizeable tributary.

Selkirk's angling association, however, seems to have the largest trout stretch; eighty miles of water covering Tweed, Yarrow and Ettrick waters. They restock the waters annually from their own hatchery.

Trout fishing tickets can also be obtained at very reasonable cost at Walkerburn, Innerleithen and Broughton.

How many fish? What size? When to catch them?

Certainly the days of Canon Greenwell's fifty-odd fish in a day are over. But between May and the end of August six to ten fish in the day is not unusual. In the main river, they come out at about 1 lb in weight, perhaps 1½ lb, whereas the tributaries such as the Jed or the Leader produce mainly half-pounders.

Although the statutory trout fishing season in Scotland is from 15 March to 6 October, this period is reduced on the main river in most places to 1 April to 30 September. My favourite period for trout on the Tweed is from mid-April to the end of May. flies? Well, when fishing downstream wet (the most popular method although not always the most profitable) I would suggest (inevitably) Greenwell's Glory, Blae and Black, Butchers and Iron Blue Dun. Hook size 12-14. Fishing dry — Greenwell's, March Brown and Tupps's Indispensible should do well.

The Tourism Division of the Borders Regional Council at Newtown St Boswells publish a booklet called 'Angling on the Scottish Borders' which costs 61p (post paid). It is an excellent guide and it shows all the waters — lochs, streams and rivers — in the Borders areas. In particular it has many pages devoted to the Tweed river system.

Tweed's bygone bonanzas

There is a fibreglass replica at the Freshwater Fisheries Laboratory near Pitlochry of one of the biggest fish of its kind ever to be caught in Britain. It was caught quite recently in the autumn of 1988 in the lower reaches of the River Tweed which, of course, makes it doubtful if it can be declared a *Scottish* monster since the Tweed is partly English and Scottish in its flow. The fish was a sea trout and it weighed 28½ lb.

Unhappily, this fish was not caught by an angler on rod and line but in nets. This is not unusual because, although sea trout on the Tweed are prolific, for some unknown reason they are notoriously difficult for anglers to catch. They are distant migrators as many of them head down the North Sea to the Norfolk and Suffolk coasts, where they feed heavily on sand eels, sprats and small herring. Some cross the North Sea and feed in areas off Holland and Denmark before returning to spawn. We know this because tagged fish have been traced. Tweed sea trout grow fast and they seldom spawn more than once or twice.

This 100-mile river flows mainly from Scotland before running into England and emptying into the North Sea at Berwick-on-Tweed. Recognised far and wide as an angler's paradise, the excellent trout found in the Tweed bring fishers in their hundreds from both sides of the border. But it is really the valuable salmon beats which command high prices in spring and autumn. Both the humble trouters, paying a few pounds for a day or a week for their sport, and the richer salmon enthusiasts, who pay thousands of pounds for the privilege of a week, think themselves fortunate if they catch either a dozen trout or one salmon a day. We hear occasionally of three or four salmon in a day but rarely much above a dozen trout. the salmon might weigh from 10 to 15 lb; anything larger is a celebration. And the trout, with the odd exception, are usually about three-quarters of a pound each.

It is interesting to compare these figures with the angling scene a hundred or so years ago. In 1853 the famous angler and author Stoddart told how the Duke of Roxburgh occasionally caught between twenty and thirty salmon and grilse in one day in the Maxwell Pool of Floors Water alone. Immediately below Kelso there is a stretch called Sprouston fishings and Stoddart described one pool, conjectured 'by those competent to judge' to contain a congregation of a thousand salmon and grilse. Then he goes on to say how Thomas Kerss fished in that pool and took out six salmon *in half an hour*, as fast, in fact, as they could be hooked and played to the bank.

Angling for trout, too, in Stoddart's time was nothing short of a bonanza. His friend John Wilson, fishing the burns which empty into the Tweed, thought nothing of catching *twelve dozen* brown trout in the course of a forenoon.

In terms of size and weight, the bygone days of the Tweed have a tantalising record for anglers who are content with today's average catches. The individual record fish for the Tweed is the well-known 69¾ lb salmon caught by Lord Home, years before official records were kept. Then in October 1886, Mr Pryor caught one of 57½ lb on Floors Water and this is the recognised Tweed record. The fish was 53 inches long and it had a girth of 20½ inches. Fifty-pounders from the Tweed were caught every few years from this time onward. Mr Brererton caught one of 55 lb in 1889, then Mr Kidson one of the same weight in 1913, and Mr Fison one of 51½ lb in 1922.

From the sublime to the ridiculous; the smallest on record is a four-year-old spring salmon — not a grilse — which weighed only 2 lb 15 ozs. It was caught by Colonel T. G. Taylor on the Tweed on 27 March 1928. Mr Arthur Hutton, an expert, examined some of the scales and said that the fish had had two years in the river and two years in the sea.

That sea trout on the Tweed are difficult to catch by rod and line is evidenced by the fact that the only outstanding monster is one of 15 lb caught by fly in November 1933. On the other hand, the record of the numbers and sizes of bull-trout is very scant but there is evidence of whole cart-loads of these cannibal fish being caught in a single night, from a short stretch of the river, many of them 5 and 6 lb in weight. The bull-trout on the Tweed was (doubtless still are) considered by anglers as great an evil as the pike because of its appetite for salmon parr. These large, voracious predators are still prolific in the river.

For over a hundred years the River Tweed has given sport and fish galore to generations of anglers, both those of modest means and the rich, and it is hardly surprising that the water is recognised as the finest for fishers in Europe.

Although the rental of rod fishings a hundred years ago were absurdly low in price, compared with today 'telephone number' prices, there were fewer anglers fishing the river than today. This may have been the reason for the larger catches and the bigger fish per angler, but commercial netting was lively and almost perpetual, to say nothing of illegal netting and spearing.

There must be other reasons for the difference. Could it be the poorer skill of today's anglers?

Land of the trout (Teviot)

There is an area of rivers, well away from the glamour and the high rents and the general genteel air of Tweed fishings which, in my opinion, is a paradise for trout anglers even though the waters have exciting pools and an excellent reputation for salmon. I mean the Tweed tributaries and in particular those south of the main river but still this side of the border with England.

This is not to say that those north of the river deserve any less praise. The Whiteadder, Blackadder, Leet, Eden, Leader, Gala and Leithen Waters speak for themselves. But the towns of Selkirk, Hawick, Jedburgh and Kelso

The River Teviot above the junction with the Tweed.

are each in the centre of angling waters that are both beautiful and prolific for trout fishermen. Even in name the Quair, Yarrow, Meggat, Ettrick, Ale and Borthwick waters are the romantic essence of the Borders. And further upstream, if the waters there were deep in the English southlands, anywhere within 100 miles of London, they would be hailed and cherished as the most highly-priced trout waters in Europe. As it is, they have enjoyed a hundred years of sparse angling population and very moderate angling prices for first-class fishing.

The greatest of these, in my opinion, is the Teviot. It is not a 'water', not a stream nor a burn nor a mere feeder for the mighty Tweed. It is a river in its own right and as such has a great share of migrating fish, resident trout and some coarse fish in its slower reaches. The Teviot rises on the high ground between Dumfries-shire and Roxburghshire and runs forty miles, during which it receives the waters of many tributaries.

In his book *The Angler's Companion to the Rivers and Lochs of Scotland* Stoddart said,

> 'Some years ago in the neighbourhood of Hownam ten or eleven miles from Kelso, my friend Mr Wilson and myself captured betwixt us thirty-six *dozen* trout of excellent quality and respectable dimensions abound.'

There is no doubt that they did count their trout in dozens-per-day in those days. And the fish were of any size from 1 to 3 lb. Then he goes on to say that sea trout up to 20 lb have been taken. The impression I get is that Stoddart and his angling friends threw back any trout less than 1 lb in weight! Yet all is not lost today in terms of comparisons. I am informed by the present secretary of one of the angling clubs who fishes the Teviot that trout of 4 lb are not at all uncommon.

Beyond Hawick and for nine miles to the north-east, Trow Burn, Dean Burn and Rule Water join the river. Then comes the Ale near Ancrum. The Teviot joins the Tweed near Kelso forming the Junction Pool, famous for its salmon catches, but before this other tributaries — the Jed, Oxnam and Kale Waters meet the river.

A visiting angler to the area will be showered with opportunities for trouting. And while his richer brethren may be salmon fishing on the exclusive beats of the Tweed and paying a fortune for a week, he can enjoy dry flying the Teviot and its tributaries in Arcadian surroundings for a few pounds for the day or for the week.

The Scottish Borders tourist people are not slow to publicise their tremendous angling assets. The Tourist Board publish a booklet 'Angling Guide to the Scottish Borders' at a moderate price which shows where tickets on a daily or weekly basis are available. The various angling associations at Kelso, Hawick and Jedburgh, as well as the fishing tacklists in these centres, gladly welcome visitors who would like to fish. And there are hotel waters with charges as low as £2 for a day's trouting right up to £270 for a week for salmon and sea trout. There is something for everyone who wants to fish in the green splendour of the Tweed's southern tributaries. And the finest of these, in my opinion, is the Teviot.

A value-for-money trout river (Whiteadder)

Angling associations and clubs come in all shapes and sizes. Some have water which they own or manage. Others have no waters and simply go on outings here and there. There are those which are more protective organisations than anything else; they employ their own river watchers and come down heavily on anyone fishing without a permit. And there are some which are *supposed* to take care of their water but which are slipshod about it, and fishing without a permit is the order of the day.

What really conditions these various types of clubs, at the end of the day, is money and the value of the fishings they control. There is a delightful river near Blair Atholl for instance, controlled by a local angling club which does not permit day tickets, does not encourage visitors and has a waiting list five years long even among local people. On the other hand, I know of a club with a good salmon river in Dumfries-shire which, in order to cut back on

The River Tummel.

overheads, has reduced the keepering to one person. The result? It is fished to death by 'anglers' with set lines and all sorts of fish-catching hardware.

Sometimes there is not much difference in value or price between a well-run angling syndicate and a hard-to-get-into club with good fishing water. In general terms, you really get what you pay for in Scottish angling. There are few 'bargains'.

There are, however, some very well managed angling associations who take the same enterprising view of visitors as do the local tourist authorities: visitors are welcome to their waters at reasonable cost, under reasonable conditions. They know the 'stranger passing through' with a fishing rod has a greater value to the local economy than might appear at first sight. This is why they make it easy for an angler to simply walk into a shop, buy a permit and start fishing, providing the angler obeys the rules in the small print on his permit.

In my opinion, the Berwick and District Angling Association is such an organisation which looks after the angling interests of the River Whiteadder. Their task, so far as visitors are concerned, is made a little simpler, of course, since the Tweed Protection Order came into force, which makes it an offence for anyone to fish without a valid permit obtained in advance.

Why on earth anyone would want to avoid paying for a fishing permit on this river is difficult to understand, considering that a day ticket costs £3.50 and a weekly ticket £5. The whole river is stocked regularly with brown trout, and a friend of mine has spent his summer holidays fishing here for over twenty years.

The Whiteadder rises 1,100 feet up in the Lammermuir Hills in East Lothian and runs into Berwickshire for over thirty miles. It changes its nationality for about a mile, just above Berwick, when it flows into English soil. At its source the Whiteadder Reservoir was built for water supply purposes, so the fishing river really starts below the reservoir at Chirnside Bridge then down by Allanton Bridge to Canty's Bridge beyond which it joins the Tweed upstream from Berwick.

The best trout fishing is by dry fly and visitors from the more pastoral sunny south of England will find a lot of the Whiteadder surroundings to their taste. Tickets are fairly easy to obtain from the Red Lion pub at Allanton, the Game Fair or Jobsons' shops in Berwick, or from the Secretary of the Association, or from the various hotels in the area of the river.

There are two parts of the river where fishing is private. One is a stretch upstream from Canty's Bridge, and the other is between Blue Stone Ford and Edington Mill. All the rest is ticket water — and in my estimation, excellent value for money for a trout angler.

A trout fairyland (Ettrick and Yarrow)

From the little town of Moffat in Dumfriesshire there is a twisty road, the A708, running east to fairyland. In my opinion this road goes through some of the most glorious scenery in the Scottish Lowlands. It really is the only feasible road from Moffat to Selkirk and, for the first few miles, it more or less follows the Moffat Water, one of the three streams which start the Annan on its course down to the Solway.

The road eventually reaches two lochs in the hills, the little Loch of the Lowes which is connected by a small burn to the longer St. Mary's Loch; both are well managed by an angling club in Edinburgh and both are regularly stocked. After passing the lochs and the ancient and famous Tibbie Shiels Inn, the road follows another stream which starts from the loch all the way down, almost to Selkirk. This is Yarrow Water which joins Ettrick Water which is a tributary of the Tweed.

To my mind, fish or no fish, this is an area of Tweedside that has all the open-sky splendour of the Borders, a country of green fells and rolling moorlands. The Yarrow river has never been taken too seriously as a salmon river, but for its brown trout fishing it is a joy just to be on the water. The Selkirk and District Angling Association stock the river annually with trout and they welcome visitors who wish to fish. The Association control eighty miles of Ettrick and Yarrow Waters as far as Lindean Bridge, and their charge for daily or weekly tickets is low.

Another six miles of Ettrick and Yarrow Waters is available to visitors, for both salmon and trout fishing, at Bowhill from the Buccleuch Estates, whose offices are at Bowhill, just outside Selkirk.

Edinburgh's 'Gardez-Loo' river (Water of Leith)

While other cities in days past had their town criers to bring together crowds to hear the latest news, the city of Edinburgh had something of the reverse. When a pedestrian walking in the Royal Mile's narrow roadway between very tall tenement buildings heard the cry from above 'Gardez-Loo' he would wisely run like mad into the nearest entrance-way or close. Then the reason for the cried warning would come down into the street from a window far up in the building — rubbish or slops or sewage. That was how the occupants of these high buildings got rid of their trash — over the windowsill — and that was the habitual morning cry heard by passers-by.

The relationship between this unsavoury bygone practise and Edinburgh city's own little river, the Water of Leith, is perhaps unfair. But it must be said that this stream, which runs twenty-four miles from the west of Harperrig Reservoir to the Forth of Leith and flowing rapidly through dense populations, was, at one time, the most industrialised and polluted river in Scotland. Thirty mills along its banks made all sorts of things from paper to snuff (some are still working), and although most are now gone many of the mill dams and weirs are still there, happily in a relatively clear and clean state.

Preston Mill on the River Tyne in East Lothian.

The Water of Leith is now a trout river, not a significant one perhaps, but attractive to young anglers or others who cannot (or do not) wish to travel far afield for their sport. Everyone can fish it free of charge as far upstream as Balerno and the fact that it gives great pleasure to about 2,000 anglers a year is due to the hard work and enterprise of Lothian Regional Council's Department of Leisure Services. They stock the river with brown trout annually and employ river watchers, part of whose job, I expect, is to prevent any 'Gardez-Loo' poachers in what is now a pleasant city stream. There is a committee of Honorary Bailiffs to advise on policy.

The trout are cautious and not too easy to catch by fly fishing and they run about four to the pound. There is a continuous walkway on the bank of the river along the old Balerno railway line and fishing is accessible from here or from Lanark Road. In the slack, smooth, stretches of the water, a big trout is occasionally caught — 1½ or 2 lb in weight.

Another Esk

If you say you are going to fish the Esk, please make sure you know which river you mean. Just think how many we have in Scotland alone — the Border Esk in Dumfries-shire, the North and South Esks in Angus and the two in Lothian called the North and South (although they are branches of one river).

The Lothian North Esk starts in the Pentland Hills and flows down through Carlops, Penicuik and Lasswade. The South Esk rises ten miles eastward. The two waters pass through a bygone industrial landscape of disused coal mines and paper mills until they join near Dalkeith in the park surrounding Dalkeith Palace.

Musselburgh and District Angling Club manage and stock the water and sea trout, as well as a few salmon, come into the tidal part

The unpretentious Almond

of the river in the spring and autumn. There is a fish ladder at Inveresk at the weir so that migrating fish can get upstream to spawn near Dalkeith.

The best trout fishing is in the lower river, starting at Montonhall Golf Course and going on for about five miles to Musselburgh where it empties into the Firth of Forth.

For all that the Lothian Esk has a difficult time retaining its dignity and beauty as a trout stream, flowing as it does through what was once one of Scotland's busiest industrial and mining areas, there are now stretches which are a pleasure to look at and to fish. Industry is a feature of life which comes and goes; rivers, like the Esk, seem to go on for ever.

Incidentally, the word Esk is simply an old Celtic word meaning 'water' from which the words Exe, Axe and Usk are derived.

A river which runs past the town of Livingston is called the Almond (not to be confused with the other Almond which is a tributary of the Earn in Perthshire). Flowing as it does through a landscape dotted by the lugs of former coal and shale oil mining, it is not a pretty river all along its length. Thanks, however, to the work of the Forth River Purification Board, Almond water does carry trout and from a point at Midcalder it is a respectable and clear fishing water, particularly as it cascades over the rocks at Almondell. Nine miles farther on it enters the Forth at Cramond, a pretty old mill village and mainly a centre for small craft sailing.

In 1978 the Almond Angling Association worked with the Lothian Regional Council to

The Nith in Dumfriesshire.

install a fish pass at Mid-Calder and sea trout now ascend to the upper spawning reaches of the river.

Dry fly fishing is popular on this small river and local anglers prefer to start at Almondell (Almondell and Calder Wood country park is nearby) and fish downsteam from there. The Association has its own hatchery and stocks the river annually.

Another popular stretch is the tidal water at Cramond, where anglers fish for sea trout and catch occasional salmon.

Mid-Calder is the focal point for brown trout anglers. Here there are two tributaries, Linhouse and Muireston waters, both of which run directly from the Pentland Hills. They are clear, sweet streams with trout.

The flies used by anglers are not unlike those from the Clyde — small and sparsely dressed with very little colouring.

The other Tyne

There is another Tyne. I did not know of its existence until I saw it on a map and talked later to the people who fish it. This Tyne is nowhere near Newcastle. From its source at Pathead, a busy ex-industrial and mining area, south-west of Edinburgh, it runs through East Lothian and flows twenty-five miles to empty into the North Sea at Tyninghame near Dunbar. During its course from the northern faces of the Moorfoot and Lammermuir Hills to the North Sea the river passes through pastoral farming country and the small towns and villages of Lothian — Gladsmuir, Haddington, Hailes and East Linton.

It would be untrue to say that this Tyne is anything else but a pretty river in places. The river is stocked with brown trout and is well managed by the East Lothian Angling Association. Certainly sea trout are caught at dusk, some around 3 lb, but the usual run is brown trout of ½ to 1 lb, in weight. Salmon are occasionally seen but few seem to get past the falls at East Linton. They are probably netted by the estate of Tyninghame.

The association issues fishing permits through fishing-tackle dealers in Edinburgh, Haddington and Dunbar. River watchers will also sell permits at the water. Most of the river is association water, although there are a few private stretches.

The river reaches a significant width between the mills at Haddington. Access to the water is simple as it runs between the A1 road and a twisting back road and it can be reached from either of these.

The Tyne trout, like those on the Clyde, are very shy, so it is advisable to fish with great stealth, fine casts and small flies size 16 or even smaller. The fun really starts when a 3 lb sea trout decides to snatch it!

The Lammermuir Hills in East Lothian where the Tyne rises.

Lomond, Stirling and the Trossachs

The rivers

Leven · Endrick · Forth · Teith · Allan · Devon

Loch Lomond and Ben Lomond.

The miracle waterway to the Bonnie Banks (Leven)

Those who have read any of the numerous books about Scotland's Loch Lomond will not be left in doubt about the glorious angling opportunities offered by the bonnie banks of the largest area of fresh water in Britain (27,45 square miles). The late Bill McEwan, and some years before him Henry Lamond, wrote books on the glories of the loch. To say the least about this mountain-fringed water, there are no fewer than twenty species of fish there including perch, grey mullet, stickleback, four-spined stickleback, ten-spined stickleback,

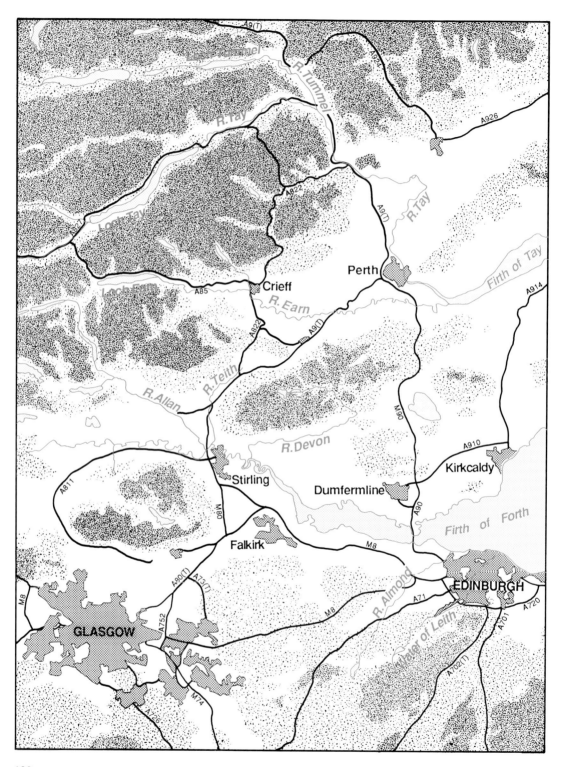

flounder, roach, minnow, tench, loach, pike, salmon, grey trout, sea trout, brown trout, powan, sharp-nosed eel, sea lamprey, and river lamprey.

The brown trout and other fish are residents of the loch; the migratory fish are salmon and sea trout and they come up the loch in shoals, usually along the Endrick Bank, to go up the rivers Endrick and Fruin to spawn.

How do they get into the loch from the sea?

The fish come up from the Atlantic Ocean into the Firth of Clyde and at the town of Dumbarton turn left into River Leven. They travel the eight miles up this 'gateway' into Loch Lomond, where they make their way to the spawning rivers that flow into the loch; the main spawning redds are in the Endrick and they are guarded carefully by the local association. Incidentally, it is only since the fourteenth

century that the loch has been called 'Lomond' a name taken from the Ben which overlooks the loch. Before that time both the river and the loch were of the same name — Leven. It is said that the ancient family name of Lennox, a familiar one in these parts, comes from 'Leven'.

The Leven is listed in angling guidebooks as 'a tributary of the Clyde'. And this is so for both the Clyde and the Leven share the same estuary. The Leven, however is much more than that to the angling community.

In one way, the River Leven is what I would call a 'miracle' river. Frankly, it is not a beautiful river. An angler who seeks quiet, pleasant country surroundings will not find them on the banks of the Leven. It is very much a workaday scene. Indeed since about 1786, industry and commerce have served the river ill by using it as a dump for every

The River Tay.

conceivable kind of pollution imaginable, particularly the effluent from adjoining dyeworks and Turkey Red factories which closed down only about thirty years ago. The Leven passes through some of the busiest but drab-looking small towns in Scotland — Renton, Bonhill, Alexandria and Jamestown.

Thanks to the untiring efforts of the Loch Lomond Angling Improvement Association, which was formed in 1860, almost all of the pollution and a great deal of the poaching have been eliminated. The reason I call the Leven a 'miracle' river is, quite simply, that as a waterway for migrating fish it has come through almost unbelievable difficulties for over 200 years, yet it has triumphed and survived as the 'feeder' for Loch Lomond year after year. If control was not enforced, the Leven would have suffered the same fate as the Clyde, which was once a prolific salmon and sea trout river and is only now, in this period of cleaner water, recovering its reputation for salmon. Incidentally, the first people to be granted fishing rights on the Leven and on Loch Lomond were the monks of the nearby community of Paisley. Although this was 700 years ago, I often feel that this bequest may have endowed the river with its 'miracle' properties of recovery!

Salmon ascend the Leven in thousands but it is the sea trout shoals that attract anglers from all over the West of Scotland during the spring and summer. Scenery or no scenery, it cannot be denied that sea trout fishing on this river yields large catches for anglers year in and year out.

In Loch Lomond itself sea trout weighing 6 lb or more are fairly common and specimens of 14 lb are sometimes taken. It was not usual for nets in the Leven and in the Clyde estuary to get fish weighing as much as 15 lb; one sea trout netted in the Leven in June 1928 weighed 19 lb. (The record Scottish sea trout weighed 21 lb and was caught in the River Awe.)

July brings the main run of sea trout up the Leven and from that time onward, till well into winter, successive shoals of fish enter the loch from the river. Many of these later running fish are 'whitling' or 'black-nebs' as they are called locally; they weigh from ¾ lb to 1½ lb.

Poaching has always been a problem on the Leven and, looking on the side of these illegal opportunists, their activities are clear evidence of the prolific runs of fish. The poaching

tradition obviously grew from a mixture of many things: proximity to heavily populated areas along the course of the river, proximity to the industrial towns of Dumbarton and the city of Glasgow, and the disastrous slump years in the 1920s which affected the Vale of Leven more than many other parts in Scotland.

Even today the watchers of the Loch Lomond Angling Association have a constant job guarding the fishings, both in the river and on the loch. During the time of the big salmon and sea trout runs, as many as seven association watchers are employed on the River Leven alone, mainly at night to catch the netters.

But for the trout and sea trout angler who wants good fishing first and scenic beauty for his surroundings second, I would recommend this short, fish-crammed gateway to Loch Lomond. Getting a permit is relatively easy. Day or weekly tickets for both the Leven and Loch Lomond cost a few pounds and can be obtained from tacklists in the area, from boat hirers on the loch, from local hotels, or directly from the association offices at 29 St Vincent Street, Glasgow G1 2DT. For those anglers who are strangers to the waters, I can recommend the fishing-tackle dealer Jim Kent at Yoker, on the west side of Glasgow, who not only sells permits for the Leven but knows every inch of the water and the flies or lures to use.

Although there is little doubt that bait fishing (grub or worm or even shrimp) is widely used on the Leven, the ardent sea trout fly fisher will not feel strange on such an excellent water. That the brown trout and sea trout are there in thousands is an assurance of a good day's fishing, if perhaps not a day in sylvan surroundings.

Sea trout at night on the Endrick

Most visitors simply run out of adjectives when they see Loch Lomond on a good day. It is Scotland's largest loch (twenty-one miles long) and only thirty miles from the largest population centre in Scotland — Strathclyde. Its scenic beauty is written about all over the world. To many Scots 'by yon bonnie banks and by yon bonnie braes' is almost a national anthem!

Only the anglers know how wonderful Loch Lomond and its tributaries can be for fishing, and only the keen student of fish life knows the names of the twenty-odd varieties of fish in its waters, ranging from the ten-spined stickle-back to the sea lamprey. Migrating fish, salmon and sea trout, come in from the Atlantic via the estuary of the Clyde, turn left at Dumbarton, ascend the River Leven and enter Loch Lomond. They travel north up the loch and then go to their spawning rivers. The Fruin and the Endrick can be properly classed as rivers. The others are merely hill streams — the Falloch which runs from Crianlarich to Ardlui for six miles, Arklet Water, which is of little value as a spawning area for Loch Lomond

fish, the Inveruglas Water and the Douglas Water.

The largest tributary entering the loch is the River Endrick, and as a sea trout water it is superb, although it must be said that most anglers who fish it have mainly the salmon in mind. Regarding brown trout, the Endrick has produced some fine catches, including that monster weighing 10 lb taken by R. King in 1964.

The migrating fish, salmon and sea trout, enter the Endrick by coming up along the famous Endrick Bank on the east side of the loch. This is a large area of deposited silt and sand swept round by the river to form a huge shallow bank which drops suddenly into the depths of the loch. This is a favourite fishing stretch for anglers in boats on the loch trolling or fly fishing for salmon and sea trout.

The River Endrick has its source in the Fintry hills in west Stirlingshire and it empties

The majesty of Scotland's waterways.

into Loch Lomond just south of Balmaha. The first few miles of the river are rocky until it reaches Fintry, where there are some very spectacularly steep falls. Then for twenty miles it flows to the loch through some wonderful pools that provide great sport for sea trout anglers on late summer evenings or at night.

The well-known angler and author W. B. Currie tells of a lady, Mrs Elspeth Mitchell, fishing in a well-known pool she owns above the village of Gartness and catching eleven sea trout and one grilse one night between 9.30 and 11.45. The total weight of her bag was 43½ lb. A good friend of mine, Douglas Nicholson, has fished this part of the Endrick for years and has had some phenomenal catches of sea trout, usually at night or in the early dawn. These Endrick sea trout can be of any size from 2 lb up to 10 lb.

Only recently another angling friend was fishing the Endrick near Drymen with a two-fly cast. He caught two sea trout on this one cast, lost the one on the dropper in the struggle but managed to net the other on the tail fly. It was a fish of 4 lb.

Loch Lomond Angling Association controls the fishings on Loch Lomond and on all its tributaries. This is a long-established and well-managed organisation employing many permanent river watchers. They are very necessary in such a large area of waters so near the high population of Clydesdale.

The big river in Scotland's heartland (Forth)

If the River Forth could speak, it would pray for the fulfilment of its happy birth to provide a smooth passage through the waters of its youth, a serene middle age and a glorious estuary loved by all anglers, like the Nith, or the Navar or the Deveron.

Sadly, it has had none of these endowments for years and years — until now. Perhaps the river's silent prayers are being answered, thanks to the angelic efforts of various associations which have been working to protect and develop game fishing on this majestic river, the fifth largest in Scotland, and its many dependent tributaries. The Forth Federation of Anglers, the Forth District Salmon Fishery Board and the Forth Fishery Conservation Trust are now beginning to see the results of their herculean task of years of fighting the two P's — poaching and pollution. Any angling writer examining the Forth would be guilty of serious neglect if he did not recognise the tremendous turnaround of fishing potential, in particular the lifetime efforts of one man, Major Clifford Burke. He was, until recently, superintendent of the Salmon Fishery Board, the only full-time employee in an organisation with responsibilities covering 1,500 square miles. It is little wonder that he was awarded the MBE. For twenty-seven years, almost single-handedly and right into his seventies, he improved the fish stocks in his area — the third largest in Scotland — by restocking and by actively combating illegal netting.

The Forth rises in Scotland's romantic heartland, the Trossachs; its birthplace is in Queen Elizabeth Forest Park in Loch Chon. Then it flows down through the mountains to Loch Ard, is joined by Duchray Water and the Kelty Water which is used by sea trout for their spawning. On its other bank the Goodie Water joins it from Scotland's only lake (all the rest are lochs), the Lake of Menteith, before it meets a river which rivals it in size and significance at this stage — the Teith. This is just before Stirling. Then on it goes to become the Firth of Forth beyond Edinburgh and to be spanned by the famous bridge. The Forth touches Fife on one bank and North Berwick on the other as it reaches the North Sea.

That is the Forth proper; strictly speaking not of outstanding interest to the angler at its birthplace in the streams behind the lochs Ard and Chon. Once it is kissed by the Teith, however, it starts to look important.

There are reasons and occasions when I am glad to be more of a trout fisher than a salmon fisher. And the Forth is one of these reasons. I must doff my cap, not only to the gallant major, but to Tom McKenzie and Sandy MacKay, secretary and treasurer of the Allan Water Angling Association at Dunblane in Perthshire. Both are members of the Forth District Salmon Fishery Board. They are typical

Stirling Castle towers over the Forth and the Teith.

of the growing number of lovers of fishing who decided to stand up and be counted in the battle described by writer James MacKie as the 'Slaughter on the Forth'. This refers to the poaching and illegal netting downstream from Kincardine bridge which has been going on for years.

On one May night Mr MacKie counted seventeen boats all drift-net fishing for salmon illegally. The situation became so bad that BBC Television and many national newspapers gave the matter considerable coverage. Questions were asked by the local Member of Parliament at the Scottish Office. The Forth Fishery Conservation Trust estimated that 20,000 fish a year valued at £250,000 were being taken illegally from the estuary.

The whole sorry business reached a climax of police attention when 11 lb of explosives were placed under the car of a former netsman who had allegedly 'grassed' to the police on other netsmen. The police then took sudden and dramatic interest in illegal netting on the Forth after that sign of terrorism! Around this time, some persons even broke into a police compound in a nearby town and stole nets which had been confiscated.

Happily for salmon anglers the situation in the estuary is now improving and every year there is better promise for the rod fisherman upstream.

What about the trout?

I can remember a time when the Forth between Dunblane and Stirling amounted to nothing very much for trout or sea trout anglers. All the attention of the trout people was focused on the excellent fishing to be had on the chain of lochs in the Trossachs that really comprise the Forth-Teith system — Venachar, Lubnaig, Voil, Achray, Katrine and Drunkie. Nowadays the increase in popularity on this stretch of the river is plain to see from the Glasgow to Stirling motorway.

During August and September sea trout fishing here is better than many people have realised. And going by the numbers of anglers seen fishing from the roadway during these months, particularly at weekends, fishers are wakening up to the improved conditions. There are also good stretches available upstream from Gartmore bridge and permits for these can be bought at the Station Buildings, Aberfoyle. Tickets for the six-and-a-half miles of river downstream from Gartmore bridge can be obtained from tackle shops in Glasgow, Kirkintilloch, Stirling and Falkirk.

It is easy to see why fishing rivers in the lowlands of Scotland have had such a hard time surviving as fishing waters. The 'industrial belt' of Scotland has always been just that; it is where most of the work was done and still is, where most of the pollution happens and, inevitably, where most of the poaching takes place. The Highlands are luckier, at least in these respects.

Yet for all the difficulties of maintaining good fishing stocks and facilities for anglers, waters in the lowlands are being managed better and better each year as the demand increases. Riparian owners, angling clubs, associations and local authorities are controlling their rivers and lochs in the heartland with good stocking policies and effective keepering.

The mighty Forth is part of this change. The signs are there for the river which is number five in Scotland in terms of size, to be much further up the league in terms of fishing potential. The pollution is decreasing in the Firth and the poaching and illegal netting is commanding more and more successful attention from the authorities. Too much is at stake for tourism and recreation to allow the fishing to be destroyed, considering the Valhalla of waters upstream that depend on the quality of water both for resident trout and for migrating fish.

The Teith . . . the river with a little of everything

Like many anglers I want a little bit of everything from a river. I like lovely surroundings, easy wading or bank fishing, a moderately-priced permit to fish, a distance that is within easy reach of the water from my home, and a reasonable chance of decent-sized fish. My wife and family might add something else that they could want — interesting places to visit if they come with me and I am up to my thighs in water most of the time.

The Teith in central Scotland is a river that has many, but perhaps not all, of those things. But I like to fish it, particularly in the early part of August because (a) the scenery is at its best towards the end of summer and (b) while fishing, especially for brown trout in rough water there is always the possibility of the 'big surprise' that makes most angler's hair stand on end when they suddenly find themselves battling with a 4 lb sea trout. Yes, it is a river of migrating fish as well as supporting a good population of resident brown trout.

The Teith is part of the Forth river system and it runs from the world-famous mountain-and-loch area of the Trossachs, the romantic lands described by Sir Walter Scott in his novels and the one-time home of Rob Roy, down through some of the most attractive mountain routes in Europe. Apart from the fishing, here is a water-course in the heart of Scotland which an angler would find a pleasure just to travel on a day in late summer. From Loch Voil the River Balvaig flows through bonnie Strathyre to Loch Lubnaig (whence comes the Leny Water) and this takes us to the town of Callander. From out of the west another water chain flows from Loch Katrine to Loch Achray and into Loch Vennacher, then to Callander to meet its brother. That is when the Teith properly starts its life as a fishery. The river meanders and rushes alternatively through rocky gorges and quiet pools past Doune, where it meets the river Forth on its way through Stirling, and thence to the North Sea.

In the heart of the Trossachs — Loch Achrray from above Loch Venachar.

This whole area of central Scotland, from Loch Lomond in the west to Edinburgh in the east, is patterned and rippled with lochs, rivers, streams and burns and nearly all of them are worth an angler's attention. And the Teith has its own distinguished place in the middle of it all as a fishing river, mainly because of its interest and beauty. Certainly it has been described as the best salmon river by far in the Forth-Teith complex. That may be so (I have never taken a salmon on this river) but its main attraction to me is its trout and sea trout angling.

Every spring and autumn, migrating fish come in from the North Sea and battle their way up the rivers on the east coast of Scotland, the better known, of course, being the Spey, the Tay, the Dee and the Tweed. Others, like the Forth, are not so well known for their fishing prospects. The Teith, as a tributary of the Forth, is one of these lesser-known waters. It joins the Forth just a few miles west of

Stirling and for years, like the Forth itself, suffered from pollution at the estuary down from Edinburgh. Now, thanks to the good efforts of the Forth Angling Improvement people, all those rivers of the Forth system have been greatly improved for salmon and sea trout runs.

Coming down from the lochs of the Trossachs, the Teith flows through the town of Callander in grand style and I have often stood looking over the bridge which spans the river on the main road to Glasgow and have seen trout and sea trout galore. Quite apart from the possibilities of getting a good catch, perhaps even a salmon, on this town water, it is an excellent area for children and beginners. Permits to fish are very moderate in price and because the river here is flanked by a small public park, casting tuition can be given without the hazard of being 'hung up' in the foliage of overhanging trees.

Serious fishing, however, is best downstream

129

from Callander. Some stretches of the river are privately owned or leased on long terms to tenants, although permits can be got on request in advance from Gart Estate, Lamrick Castle, Blair Drummond and Ochertyre Estates. The best plan for a visiting angler is simply to see Jimmy Allan, of the fishing-tackle shop 'James Bayne' in Main Street, Callander, or Mrs Neil, of Messrs Crockhart, in King Street, Stirling.

The village of Deanston, a few miles from Callander, has a local malt whisky distillery by an excellent stretch of the Teith. It is possible on application to them to get a permit to fish this beat, although most permits are granted to the residents of Deanston village. The hotels in Callander or Strathyre will arrange fishing for an angler if he stays for a night or two, and that is a very good idea if he wants to give his family a pleasant few days' holiday. Then there is the popular Blue Bank fishing between Callander and Dunblane, and the Cambusmore stretch of the river which I have sampled profitably many times. These are private beats with a limited number of fishers allowed on each beat.

Depending on the ever-important factor of water temperature, sea trout run on the river as early as the end of March, thus competing for insect life and other food with brown trout, which are active right from opening day on 15 March.

Drawbacks for the angler on the Teith? Yes, like most rivers one way or another, there are a few which I have experienced. I found in most areas that the wading was a slippery activity. Perhaps I was just unfortunate in my search for nice, gentle, shingle shores although I must say that the beat owned by the whisky distillery at Deanston had a very attractive shoreline of sand and pebbles on the south bank. On all my other trips I was very glad to use my wading stick on those large, slippery boulders.

I observed another problem on at least one part of the river, namely the proximity of the river to the road, particularly between Deanston and Callander. Access to good areas of fishing was freely available to anyone who cared to stop at one or other of the prepared parking spaces under the trees. And since this part of the lower Highlands is only within a few miles of highly populated towns and cities, the invitation to fish illegally and poach is obvious. Indeed I know this to be a fact of life, as I

heard the complaints of the water bailiff in the area.

For all these minor irritations, the Teith is a very good fishing river with a bit of everything an angler and his family could want.

For the non-anglers, this whole area of Scotland near the River Teith is festooned with walks and drives and castles and places to visit. There is the Achray Forest Drive, a scenic trip through Forestry Commission roads four miles north of Aberfoyle, giving magnificent views of the Trossachs, and three miles away the David Marshall Lodge, a starting point for walks in the Queen Elizabeth Forest Park commanding wide views of the whole of the Teith river valley down to the upper Forth. There is Doune Castle and nearby Doune Motor Museum, both within a mile or so from Blair Drummond Safari Park. Dunblane Cathedral (thirteenth century) is not far away, nor is Inchmahome Priory, set in the middle of Scotland's only lake, the Lake of Menteith, where Mary Queen of Scots was held in refuge.

The Teith is indeed a Scottish lowland river which is ideal for the trout or sea trout angler with a conscience about what his family can do while he is fishing. It is moderate in everything — cost of fishing, level of water, ease of access. Only one thing will occasionally give the angler a shock now and then, and a pleasant one at that, the thump of a large brown trout (recently one of 4 lb was caught) or a sea trout (recently taken — one of 6 lb). The brown trout was caught at the end of a calm pool; the sea trout (and this is typical in summer) was caught right in the torrent of rough white water. These are the kinds of experiences awaiting the avid Teith trouter.

A river from the Ochils (Allan)

Rivers change. It is not merely the ravages of wild, torrential winters changing the banks and channels of the water that signify big alterations to a fishing river. These are usually the year-by-year changes that go on all the time, creating new feeding and resting areas or removing old ones for both migrating and resident fish.

The changes which can alter the whole face of an angler's river are the ones which follow man's work. The Clyde at Glasgow was once the mainstay of salmon netters for their livelihood and it is no accident of design that a salmon is the centrepiece of the City of Glasgow's coat of arms. Then a hundred years of industry destroyed the fishing and the river became, among other excellent descriptions, a polluted water-course for much of the world's big ships. Now that the ships and the pollution have gone, the salmon is again returning to the Clyde in considerable numbers.

Such changes occur, too, in the smaller rivers and this is particularly true in the more densely populated areas of mid-Scotland and towards the east of the industrial belt. Happily, many of these rivers are 'coming back', after years of neglect or abuse, to become respectable angling waters. A typical example is Allan Water, a small river in the Forth river system and a tributary of that big waterway which goes down to spread out in majesty beyond Edinburgh.

Looking through some of the early books about angling in Scotland, written by reliable and well-respected authors, and trying to get a correct picture of a particular river depends to a large extent on the date the book was written. *The Highland Sportsman and Tourist*, by Robert Hall, describes the Allan as a beautiful river owned and cared for by a number of eminent proprietors such as Lord Abercromby, Sir J. M. Stirling-Maxwell, Sir James Alexander and Captain the Honourable A. Drummond. That was in 1860 and the impression of the river is one of a privately-held fishing stream which gave unlimited access to the thousands of salmon and sea trout coming up past Stirling from the Forth to spawn.

Fifty years later W. L. Calderwood in his book *The Salmon Rivers and Lochs of Scotland* states quite bluntly he hopes 'that better days are in store for the Allan Water.' The reasons for his dismay are the obstructions caused by

The River Endrick near Drymen.

no fewer than ten dam dykes which check the salmon and sea trout heading for the final stages of their spawning runs. These dykes or weirs in a small river in such a heavily populated area near Stirling attracted poachers galore who got their fish by stroke-hauling and other illegal methods. The dykes were built to supply water to meal and paper mills along the river and there was one woollen mill, also with a weir, which discharged various shades of blue and purple dyes into the water.

In those days, it was obvious that salmon and sea trout ready for spawning had a tremendous struggle to surmount all the weirs and dykes on the river before they could get to the redds upstream. Indeed, so difficult was the task for both kinds of fish that they were baled out by the bailiffs of the District Salmon Board with some helpers and transferred to the upper water so that they could spawn.

Going much further back in history, it would be interesting to know how the Romans treated the Allan since there is clear evidence of their stay in this part of Scotland. The remains of a Roman fort and a camp, beside what is left of the old Roman road, can be seen at Braco.

Strolling along the bank and fishing the Allan today gives an angler the impression of a river having a breathing spell and gratefully resting after a century or more of man's misuse of the water. Certainly around Greenloaning it is a quiet water and although it must be said that the water bailiff has his work cut out for him by the constant vigilance he has to exercise on poachers, it is a fine little river to sit beside or to fish.

The river rises on the Ochil Hills and runs for twenty miles through lovely Strathallan to empty into the Forth near Stirling. It is only when it is joined by the Knaik River at Greenloaning that it becomes 'of age' in size and potential for the fisher. From here down to Dunblane, the water is quite slow and very good for trouting. Then after Dunblane it becomes turbulent and fast, providing some good spots for sea trout fishing in the shallows in the evenings.

Two bodies have mainly been responsible for bringing the Allan up to its present standard for good fishing — the Forth District Fishery Board and the Allan Water Angling Improvement Association. There is a considerable restocking programme for both salmon and trout and a new and healthy respect by anglers in the area. All fishing is by permit and these can be obtained from hotels and tackle shops in Stirling, Dunblane and Greenloaning; the prices of the tickets are very reasonable at a few pounds for the day or the week.

The Allan drains seventy-seven square miles of hillsides in the Ochils and near its source is Carsbreck Loch, a water recommended not only for the excellence of its trout fishing by boat (a trout weighing 4½ lb was caught recently) but because when it is covered with ice in winter, it is sometimes used for the famous curling festivals called Bonspiels.

As far as fishing is concerned, a river can change for the better or for the worse. In these days when so many anglers complain that their favourite river 'is not what it was at all' or that 'it was far better in my father's time', it is refreshing to come across an angler's river which is being cared for and improved steadily year by year.

A river with a new lease of life (Devon)

Do not believe all you hear about fishing rivers not being what they once were; that the fishing was far, far better fifty years ago or that the fishing is now being ruined on certain rivers because of one or other of the three 'P's' — pollution, poachers and predators. Of course this gloomy view does apply to some rivers in Scotland. Who can deny that either poachers or pollution will magically go away no matter what government regulations say.

What you don't hear so much about, even along the angling community, are the rivers which are *improving*. This is particularly true in what used to be the Scottish industrial belt. Memories are short and too many of us have not looked at our history books for years to see just what it was like on some of the rivers in central Scotland. Some of them, including the Clyde where salmon are now returning, were nothing more than sewers for burgeoning

On the Teith near Callander.

towns and cities riding on the boom of the Industrial Revolution.

Today this area in the lowlands of Scotland is rapidly changing scene. The coal mining industry is in steep contraction and mines are closing all over the place. Heavy industrial plants no longer exist. Populations are moving outwards from cities and towns, and green fields, forest parks and recreation areas now replace what were workaday places.

Added to this is the valiant and skilful work undertaken by conscientious angling clubs and associations, with the help of the river purification boards, and many rivers once abandoned to industrial mill dams and weirs and effluence are now running sweetly and untinged. What is more important, they now support game fish; some already have salmon and sea trout ascending to spawn.

Typical examples of such rivers are those tributaries of the mighty Forth which empty into the North Sea beyond Edinburgh. One of these is the last one to join the Forth before it become a firth — that is the Devon.

In 1909, Calderwood gave this river scant mention in his book and as recently as 1981 it was hardly considered as a fishing river, certainly for salmon.

Now the Devon is a water well worth visiting. In its upper reaches, it runs through lovely country near Dollar and the trouting here is a joy. The water comes from Glendey and Gairney burns join the river.

Farther downstream there is reasonable sea trout fishing and the tackle man in Alloa tells me that this Devon Angling Association stretch is excellent on late summer evenings. One drawback, he says, are the overhanging trees and bushes. However, this gives the angler plenty of good practise in side-casting and sometimes plenty of reward with 2 lb sea trout or lesser size finnock.

The picturesque town of Dollar, near which the Devon flows.

The Solway

The rivers

Annan · Nith · Border Esk · Water of Fleet · Urr ·
Water of Luce · Cree

The author fishing his favourite stretch of the Annan near Johnstonbridge.

The Annan . . . an angler's hideaway paradise

The M6 motorway runs north from England to become the high road to Scotland. Tourists who may have hired a car in London or somewhere else in the south, move in steady streams all summer to 'do' Scotland. Most of them want the Scotland of the brochures . . . the tartan-festooned Highlands, the mountains and glens of bagpipe-skirling dreams.

Anglers who come north for a week or so's fishing are usually no different. With the exception of the dedicated Tweed fishers who reserve expensive beats on that world-famous river on the Borders, most salmon anglers head north at least to the Tay and more likely to the Spey in the north-east, the Oykel in Ross-shire, or even to the Helmsdale to emulate the high and mighty on royalty's favourite fishing river.

Perhaps this is why the rivers that flow into

Going for July sea trout on the Annan.

the Solway Firth on the western border of England and Scotland are so rarely appreciated by anglers from England and abroad. The Luce, the Bladenoch, the Cree, Fleet, Dee and Urr are perhaps too far west in Galloway to tempt them when they are hurrying north to their particular Valhalla. All of them are excellent trout and sea trout rivers.

Of all the Solway rivers, my favourite is the Annan, which is so much more accessible even to the hurrying fishers from the south. Indeed the river is almost alongside the main trunk road just over the Scottish border at Johnstonbridge. I first 'discovered' it many years ago when my family and I stopped overnight in the little town of Moffat on the way up from England. I bought a permit to fish the upper reaches of this river for the evening. It was a superb summer evening and I came back to the hotel with a full creel and a contented spirit that rose-coloured night.

For anglers like me who prefer quiet, pastoral surroundings, these few miles just down from the source are our kind of water. It is not a river of roaring, tumbling torrents, although it does have its moments in spate conditions simply because there is no intervening loch from source to mouth and big spates are common in the rainy season. But most of the time in the trout season it is a river of peaceful, tree-lined beauty.

The river rises not very far from the sources of the Tweed and the Clyde in the hills behind the Devil's Beef Tub near Moffat, and it runs through Dumfries-shire to the Solway at the town of Annan. I have fished only a few of its thirty-five miles, at the meeting of the source waters of Moffat, Evan and Annan and the stretches at Wamphrey, Hoddom and Applegirth. Midway down the river there are two tributaries which feed the Annan — the Ae and the Kinnel. The main river is not fast-flowing and this makes it ideal in places for trout and sea trout fishings on late summer evenings. The Annan Angling Club manages the fishings from the Annan road bridge to the estuary; daily or weekly tickets can be obtained from the club's own premises in High Street, Annan. Newbie Estates have the water from Newbie Cauld to the road bridge and although permits were once sold to visitors for this excellent beat, it is now fished on a time-share basis.

Angling friends tell me that I miss the best of it by not going to Lockerbie to fish the Kindly Tenants' stretch which is managed by the tenants of the Royal Four Towns Association of Highgate, Greenhill, Heck and Smallhome. (They were granted the four miles of fishing for salmon by King Robert the Bruce for their support in his battles with the English in the fourteenth century.) I will take their word for it and leave it there.

My favourite stretch is from Wamphrey down to Applegirth water. I like friendly nature in my fishing environment and an angler would have to be very insensitive not to be enchanted with quiet glides and babbling waters that run through this countryside — and to hear the sounds of such a variety of birds.

Brown trout are always there, of course, as the river is regularly stocked by both the Upper Annandale Angling Association and by the Annandale Estate for their area. The old favourites of Greenwell's Glory, Grouse and Claret and the Silver Butcher invariably got me a bag or two in May and early June.

From mid-June to mid-July the fun starts with sea trout, and that is a different kettle of fish, as they say. The stretch at Applegirth above the farmer's iron bridge at Lochbrow becomes very productive, particularly on a clear, warm evening when using flies that attract those voracious fish from their dark hideaways under the trees — Teal and Silver, Blue Zulu and Bloody Butcher. Standing there like a heron and casting silently in purple silhouette into the far tree-lined bank is, in my opinion, an angler's paradise. Waiting for and then getting that gentle pull . . . then the stronger chug . . . than the rod-bending thrill of a 3 lb fish fighting like a dervish . . . that to me is the real attraction of the Annan in summertime.

I can well understand the aversion of some anglers to the use of bait on well respected sea trout rivers like the Annan — even when there is a full head of water. Fly fishing is fly fishing and even if an angler is not a purist in these

matters, worming or the use of grub or maggot is often anathema to them. For all this, and I agree with much of it, there is no doubt that in spate conditions worming or spinning is the most practical method for catching fish. Incidentally, it might be useful to read the relevant paragraph from the fishing permit issued by the estate people for the Annandale Fishing Club:—

'Ground bait is strictly prohibited. No worm fishing for salmon until the 1st of May and from then only in flood conditions i.e. when the water level is not below the white line mark on the bridges. Only fly fishing allowed for trout, sea trout and herling during April and September; from May to August inclusive spinning and worming for these is allowed only when the water level is not below the white line marked on the bridges. From April to September inclusive spinning for salmon is allowed only when the water level is not below the white line marked on the bridges. No prawn fishing is allowed at any time.'

A few months ago I was in the bar of the Red House Hotel at Wamphrey chatting to three anglers who had permits for the association stretch at Applegirth. There had been no rain for weeks and that day was even hotter and drier than the others; the water was very low on the river. These anglers had been out the previous night fishing from 10 o'clock till 2 am and between them caught seven sea trout (the largest weighed 4 lb) and two grilse. I asked them how they did it. One of them said, 'Fishing two flies on a cast and a maggot on the tail fly.'

Maggot fishing, even one on the tail fly, has never appealed to me. The wretched things snap off on the back-cast; it is difficult to get them, or cultivate them, or even keep them as maggots before they turn to bluebottles. And anyway my wife runs in horror at the sight of them! Yet there was the result; on a summer night, in four hours, in extremely low water, when other anglers did not even go to the river.

To get the best of a fishing holiday in upper Annan, an angler has the choice of waiting till autumn for those big salmon (and late autumn can bring all kinds of chilly weather) or catching the sea trout runs in June and July —

perhaps into the first few days of August. Frankly I prefer the latter. Angling then is usually more comfortable, even at night, and there is not much doubt about the sporting challenge of a fight with a sea trout.

Since the Upper Annandale Angling Association took over the Applegirth water from the Crown Agents a few years ago, the reputation of the river for fishing has gone up considerably. I can remember another evening in the local hotel bar at Wamphrey recently when I counted thirty anglers all buying tickets for that evening and night session in July. These were the 'all-night' men, expert trout and sea trout anglers whose numbers increase every year. Yet there is always plenty of fishing space for everyone. I can never remember meeting more than two anglers on any stretch I have fished.

The price of a fishing session on the Annan is within the range of most anglers' pockets; at the time of writing it is a few pounds for the week. The Red House Hotel sells tickets for two beats, the one belonging to the association and for the estate waters.

There are forty-seven fishing proprietors on the thirty-five miles of the Annan and its tributaries. Annandale Estates on the upper part of the river controls five-and-a-half miles and the estate office is at the village of St. Ann's, not far from Lockerbie and Johnston-bridge. The trout and sea trout season is from 15 April to 15 September.

This area of Dumfries-shire is particularly beautiful and the little towns like Moffat and Lockerbie are ideal tourist centres for the whole of the Scottish Borders. The little winding road between Moffat and Selkirk, for instance, is famous for its Highland-like scenery and the area through which it passes at St Mary's Loch and Loch of the Lowes are superb for picnics and moorland walks. The way down to Dumfries, on either side of the main A74, is dotted with history-laden villages and little country roads. An angler need have nothing on his conscience when he leaves his wife and family to their own resources for a few days in Upper Annandale.

For beginners to the 'gentle art', I would certainly recommend the River Annan. Apart from the low-hanging summer foliage over most far banks (these are the ones which generally manage to ensnare a mis-cast of flies), nearly all the stretches from Moffat downstream are safe, easy for wading and ideal for teacher-and-pupil fishing. My first ever brown trout was caught on the Annan and when I promoted myself to go after sea trout in the evenings, the thrill of these newly-learned experiences never left me.

Trouting in Hoddom (Annan)

I once caught a goldfish on the Annan. It was a beauty, weighing about a pound and virtually gleaming with the colour of the sunshine. It took my fly in the early afternoon – a No. 12, a tatty old Cow Dung — and as I fetched it to my net I could not help thinking; 'My little goldfish, you've certainly come down in the world going for a fly *that* colour.' Of course, I released it unharmed back into the river and wondered how long it might survive. Probably a long time.

That area of the Annan at Hoddom is famous for other fish besides salmon, sea trout and brown trout. There is some excellent coarse fishing around here and, let no one forget it, the former British record chub, a superb fish of over 10 lb, was caught on this stretch of the river. So it is likely my little goldfish, which is of the carp family, may still be swimming out his old age with his friends.

I asked the gamekeeper, 'How did *that* get in the river?'

'Oh, it happens,' he said. 'It's not the first time I've seen goldfish here. And, they'll go for a fly, believe me'.

'Maybe it thinks it's somebody dropping ants eggs into its water'.

'Maybe. It always happens after a heavy flood.' He pointed upstream. 'Y'see, up there the people who have houses by the riverside have big gardens that go right down to the river. And some of these gardens have fish-ponds in them containing goldfish. So when there's a heavy spate, the river sometimes rises to flood the gardens'.

Sunset on the Annan in Dumfriesshire.

'And the goldfish get out?'

'Right.'

'Did you see the fly he went for?' I showed him my disgraceful, half-chewed old Cow Dung fly.

'Mh'. He examined it. 'They usually like a Grouse and Claret, size 14'.

Although my customary and much-loved stretch of the Annan is many miles upstream at Wamphrey and Johnstonbridge, I must say how impressed I was by the Hoddom Castle Beat. The river here flows gently, sweetly and is big enough to accept those casts that are full of hope and glory where the white water flows out to become such splendid pools. And the fish are there, most certainly. Brown trout fishing in early summer, followed by those balmy summer nights after sea trout makes Hoddom, especially the middle beat, an angler's dream.

As is usual in good salmon water, the brown trout at Hoddom are considered a bonus and it is not unusual for a salmon angler to hook one on a smallish fly. The best brown trout recently caught weighed 6 lb 9 oz.

Sea trout are another matter. Anglers who go for this Prince of Fish on the Annan, as on other Border rivers, fish in the deep sunset or at night. A sea trout of 11 lb was caught recently but generally fish weighing 2 lb and, of course, herling of ¾ lb are taken. Fishing for sea trout here is a single-purpose job and when one is caught in the gloaming in one of the many deep, dark runs under the trees, you may be sure it is not a stray which happened to take an interest in a passing salmon fly.

The Hoddom part of the Annan is a well-managed and reasonably priced fishing. They only allow fifteen rods per day on the stretch and the charge per day is under £10. Wading is fairly easy, providing an angler remembers that there are shelves of sandstone under the gravel and watches out for pot-holes. Night fishing for sea trout really demands a thorough reconnaissance of the beat by day to establish where the hazards in wading may be.

The Annan is a border river which runs from the Devil's Beef Tub, about a mile from the source of the Tweed, and it courses down thirty miles through the rich farmlands of Dumfries-shire to empty into the Solway Firth at the town of Annan. It is by no means a river of the moorland wilderness or the Highland mountains. The feeding for trout and sea trout, therefore, is plentiful and sometimes during a spate when the water is coffee-coloured, the best offering for these fish is the worm.

Naturally, the Hoddom beat of the river and for some miles up-river, attracts more salmon anglers than others, particularly in the autumn. Their optimism is justified considering the river's record. Upstream in the town of Locker-bie in the Public Reading Room, there is a cast of a salmon of 51½ lb. There is record, too, of a salmon weighing 60 lb that was caught in the Sand Pool, Mount Annan, by a local minister named the Reverend A. Cook. On the Hoddom Castle water itself a 48-pounder was taken on fly in the Scales Pool.

But trouting on the Annan at Hoddom is my big attraction and better summertime angling can hardly be imagined.

The river that came back from the dead (Nith)

A lot was happening in Europe in 1812. France went to war with Russia in June of that year and, by October, the Russians had burned Moscow and Napoleon led his beaten armies in retreat across the wastes against an onsetting winter.

Something else of importance was happening in Britain. A poacher called Jock Wallace caught a salmon on the River Nith in Scotland at a place called Barjag in Dumfries-shire then had the audacity to take it to the Laird in the 'big house' to have it weighed. It was 67 lb. He fought the fish from eight in the morning till six at night and it is reported that he was down to the last two strands of his horse-hair cast, all the others being frayed in the struggle.

Although this happened before there were properly authorised fish records in Britain, a salmon of this weight exceeded the recorded top-weight fish caught in 1922 by Miss Georgina Ballantyne on the Caputh stretch of the River Tay.

Anyone with an interest in Scottish fishing waters might imagine that with this early record of a monster from the Nith, the river would have the promise of a glorious future. Yet this was not to be. Years of pollution from the mills around Dumfries, plus the general neglect of riparian owners, depleted the fish stocks so badly that as late as 1921 only a dozen or so salmon were caught in the season — to say nothing of brown trout and sea trout which were almost non-existent. Augustus Grimble in his work *The Salmon Rivers of Scotland* said this,

> '. . . It is full of pike and grayling, which ought to be destroyed as far as possible, but the proprietors appear to take no interest in the river, few of them being anglers. For the last seven years it has been going back yearly, and 1900 was the very worst on record, and not a dozen fish killed on the whole river.'

In 1934, the Nith Fishings Improvement Association was formed and in that year, so far as sea trout is concerned, a mere 273 were caught. Subsequent affiliation of the Dumfries and Galloway Angling Association, the Mid-Nithsdale Angling Association, the Upper Nithsdale Angling Association, the Dumfries Town Council and the Nith Estuary Proprietors of Salmon Netting, resulted in steps being taken to control the pollution. The whole picture gradually changed. By 1958, nearly 4,000 sea trout were caught. In 1966, 9,500 were caught and although this figure fell through the 1970s, the rod-catch of both sea trout and brown trout in this once-derelict river is now very impressive. Certainly the suspension of netting in Burgh Waters have had a lot to do with the remarkable turnaround but, most importantly, the control of pollution has allowed the shoals of finnock and sea trout to get upstream to spawn.

There is a lesson here, I feel, for other riparian owners and angling associations who

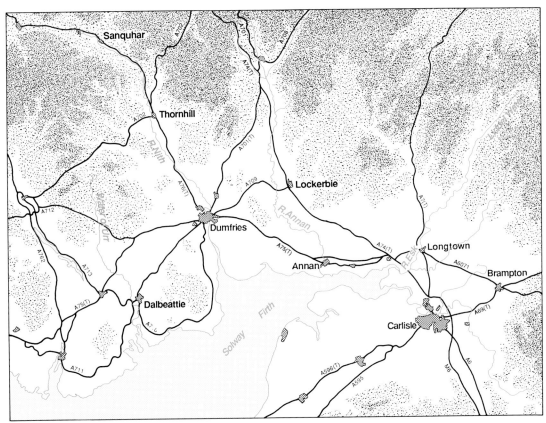

are determined to improve their fishings. It seems to me one of the wonders of nature that a river, once pollution is moderated, can recover itself within a few years to support a game fish population as has the Nith.

The Nith is the largest of the Dumfries-shire rivers and it rises in South Ayrshire near Dalmellington and runs fifty miles to the Solway Firth. During its course, it receives water from many tributary burns and smaller rivers, the chief one being Cairn Water which runs from beyond Moniaive to become Cluden Water before it enters the main river just above Dumfries. Farther upstream at Penpoint there is Scar Water, Tynron and Shinnel Waters, all feeding the Nith. Farther upstream yet at Sanquhar there are other tributaries, all of which are respectable fishing waters.

Sea trout and brown trout fishing permits for visitors can be obtained at various points along the river, usually on a weekly basis and conditional on the angler spending that time in the district. For my part, the area I recommend is at Thornhill in mid-Nithsdale. In summer, sea trout fishing here is superb, particularly in the dusk of a warm evening. The river can be reached comfortably and easily from three or four good points just outside the village and the main hotel will issue permits and give excellent advice to a visitor. What has always impressed me about the printed permits issued at Thornhill is how explicit and clear they are. They seem to be a reflection of the precise and careful management of the river, giving even the hook sizes permitted and a clear map showing exactly where the angler can fish.

In 1934 only 273 sea trout were caught, then by 1966 the figure for that year was almost 10,000. Today the annual figure is a more moderate one — around 4 to 5,000. The salmon figures have shown the same trends.

I have pleasant memories of fishing the Nith around Thornhill when I used to motor over there by way of the Dalveen Pass. On one occasion I took my two children and we witnessed something remarkable and even historical — one of the last ceremonial otter hunts in Britain. Although we were spared the spectacle of actually seeing an otter being hunted or killed, we watched the procession of liveried and uniformed people crossing the bridge led by a many-splendoured gentleman on horseback who occasionally blew on a small trumpet. At the feet of the hunters trailed a dozen or so hounds who excitedly scampered along the river bank, fortunately with more noise and acrobatics than anything else. A local villager standing beside us explained who and what they were. I was very glad for the sake of my children that they apparently found no otters that morning. I understand such hunts are now banned by law.

At New Cumnock on the Nith there is brown trout fishing and tickets are available from the local association. Then farther down at Sanquhar, there is fishing for salmon, sea trout and brown trout but only if the visiting angler stays in the district for a few days and has a ticket of introduction from his own angling club. Farther down still at Thornhill, fishing for all three species of fish is available and the Buccleuch Estates, whose office is in the village, have three beats which they let on a weekly basis. At Dumfries, tickets are available from two sources, the Nithsdale District Council and the Dumfries and Galloway Angling Association, which has a limited number of permits available; in each case advance arrangements are recommended.

Apart from the obvious good sense of controlling the fishings on the Nith by the various associations, the problem of poaching has been prevalent for many years on the river. This and simple illegal fishing without a permit has compelled associations to lay down strict rules but the visiting angler, if he obeys these, can have nothing but excellent sport on this river that came back from the dead.

The international sea trout (Border Esk)

I obtained the most authoritative and reliable fishing guidebook in Britain and searched through the Scottish section in vain for infor-mation about the Border Esk. The river rises in Dumfries and Galloway, flows into the Solway Firth and all its main tributaries are Scottish, but the reason why I could not find it in the book was because it was classed as an *English* river.

I will not argue, least of all with the editor of the 'bible' of fishing information. Another reason why I will not enter into any dispute on the matter is that others wiser and with much more clout than me, already fought the battle a few years ago. The channel of the rivers Esk and Eden flowed into the Solway; then for some natural reason it shifted towards the Scottish border. English haaf net fishermen — these are the people with the huge hand-wielded nets — who had been issued with permits by the English authority, the North West Water Authority, followed the new water route of the salmon and began fishing in what was now Scottish waters. Naturally there was a dispute and the only way they could resolve the matter was to raise a legal action. It was a fairly typical border conflict except that, on this occasion, the territorial problem was on *water* and was about the migrating course of fish. The Court of Session in Edinburgh said that the waters were in fact Scottish but by the time the action appeared in court the channel had shifted back again! Today the fishermen fish in peace in their own undisputed waters. And the fish are international.

I have always found it remarkable that while some Scottish rivers like the Aberdeenshire Dee are prime salmon waters and seem to support hardly any sea trout worth mentioning, other rivers are predominately sea trout waters that also have salmon. And why do some rivers, like the Tay, which are famous for salmon also support a large brown trout population? Others do not. In some the reason is easy to understand if we examine the food potential; in others it is not.

I always think of the Border Esk as primarily a sea trout river. In early summer sea trout fishing on this river, depending on weather conditions, can be nothing short of phenomenal. And the time for an angler to get the best sport is at night. Unless there is a spate, the water of the Esk is usually gin-clear and the way to fish it is silently, stealthily and with great patience. Field Marshal Montgomery once said that time spent in reconnaissance is never wasted, and this is particularly true for the night angler on a river like the Esk. The thing to do is to 'walk the beat' in the daytime and 'read' in preparation for the night foray. Here are things to consider on the Esk:

1. Where are the obvious sea trout areas?
2. If you intend to fish the tail of the pools, where is the best place to stand so that your cast will reach where the fish are feeding?
3. What is the back-casting situation? Will your flies be caught up in the foliage?
4. Is wading safe? Are there pot holes or deep crevices under the surface?
5. Where best can you net your fish once it is hooked?

There is one other question the angler should ask before deciding to fish at night — is it permitted? Certain stretches of the Esk and its tributaries, the Liddle, White Esk, Ewes, Wauchope and Tarras, are managed by a very vigilant Esk and Liddle Fisheries Association and there are certain restrictions at certain times about night fishing. An angler must appreciate that legitimate fishing in the darkness makes it all the more difficult for water bailiffs to identify and catch poachers. If night fishing is forbidden on any part, a thoroughly good second-best is to fish in the early morning or into the deep dusk.

Who was it who said to me that when fishing for sea trout in summer, you cannot have your fish and your sleep? You must choose.

The average weight of sea trout caught on the Esk is about 2 lb, although anglers catch them occasionally as heavy as 5 or 6 lb. Small sea trout flies fished deep at the end of the pools in the fading light of sunset produce the heavier fish.

The Broomhorn water of the Border Esk below Langholm.

In this part of Scotland the name for the finnock (a virgin sea trout on its first spawning run) is the 'herling' and the Esk is famed for its run of these in June and July.

Many visitors who motor from England intending to fish in Scotland seem to imagine that the farther north they go, the better will be the fishing. Once past the Tweed, without doubt there is a Valhalla of Scottish rivers and lochs in the Trossachs and deeper into the Highlands and in Aberdeenshire, like the Dee and the Tay. But what these eager anglers often ignore are the splendid fishing opportunities just over the Scottish border in Dumfries and Galloway and in other beautiful areas around the Solway Firth. These Solway rivers, the Nith, Cree, Dee, Annan, Urr and the Esk, have salmon, sea trout and brown trout fishing to equal any in the country. The prices of permits are reasonable and access for motorists coming from England is much easier and less time-consuming than travelling to the Highlands.

The Border Esk is one of those excellent rivers. It is formed mainly by the joining of the White Esk from the Ettrick Hills and later the Black Esk which flows from a reservoir in Dumfries-shire. On its way down to Langholm it is joined by many tributaries — Meggat Water, Ewes Water and Wauchope Water, then, later, Tarras Water. However, the Esk's main tributary is Liddle Water which flows through Newcastleton to join the Esk below Cananbie. Then the river changes its nationality and becomes English for a brief spell a little above Longtown. It flows into the Solway a few miles north of the Eden.

The three principal centres for sea trout fishing are at Cananbie, Langholm and Wasterkirk, and the best of sea trout fishing begins at the junction of the Black Esk at Langholm. The total course of the river is forty miles.

No day tickets are issued by the association and, of course, since it is a salmon river, there is no fishing on Sundays. An 'all waters' ticket on a weekly or season basis can be had at Langholm that entitles an angler to fish the Esk and its tributaries. At Netherby there are private stretches and permits for these are available at the Netherby Estates Office.

Danish sea trout in Scotland (Fleet)

Down in the south-west, tucked in cosily among the many bays and inlets along the Solway coast, is the very charming little village of Gatehouse of Fleet which, of course, takes its name from the River Fleet. It is a small river and every time I read descriptions of it, I just love to detect the faint sigh from angling authors who reluctantly admit that it is more of a sea trout river than a salmon one.

The Fleet starts its life away up in the lovely and wild Galloway hills and is formed by two tributaries, the Big Water of Fleet and Little Water of Fleet. The forest and moorland places that nurse these and other fan-patterned tributaries are more redolent of the Scottish Highlands than an area so far south — Craigie Linn, Burnfoot, the Doon of Culreoch and the Scrogs of Drumruck.

It is a lovely river in a lovely countryside, flowing at times through a splendid, planned woodland, and somehow seems a more appropriate haven for the thousands of sea trout which ascend it every summer. The Cally and the Rusko Estates own and control most of the river fishings and the former has a particular reputation for the improvement of sea trout fishing by the planting of fry from Denmark, from the island of Bornholm.

The onset of two environmental hazards in the area of Galloway has recently worried the angling community there. The first is acid rain, which has markedly affected lochs like Loch Fleet in the hills, the second is afforestation drainage, causing a loss of the 'sponge' effect on the river. For all this, the Fleet is still a good little sea trout water and, like its Solway brothers the Dee and the Cree which flank it to the east and to the west, it is very popular with anglers and reasonable in price to fish.

The steadily improving Urr

Don't imagine that the last news you received about a river and its fish is valid today. Rivers change and so do the fish which frequent them. A mere twenty years ago, who in his right mind would dream of fishing anywhere around Glas-

the Solway, was much of a sea trout river. That was until the secretary of Dalbeattie Angling Association put me right. A recent sea trout caught on the river at Castle Douglas weighed 9 lb and an average size for these fish in the river is 2 to 3 lb. The brown trout fishing, too, is fair, with fish of ½ to 1½ lb coming out to anglers' flies.

The Urr is bigger than it seems in the lower reaches. It is a river thirty-five miles long that begins up in Loch Urr. The Urr flows down

A fine catch of Sea Trout.

gow for salmon either on the Clyde or on any of its tributaries, with the notable exception of the Leven flowing out of Loch Lomond? Yet here we are today talking about who owns the salmon and sea trout fishing rights on the White Cart and the Gryfe and even the notoriously smelly Kelvin. Some extinct ship-building yards even have their oars in these contentious waters!

I never imagined that the River Urr, which runs away down in the south of Scotland into

through Dalbeattie into Rough Firth, which is one of the numerous inlets of the Solway Firth. It is a moorland water from the time it leaves the loch, then it slows down as it reaches the tidal water beyond Dalbeattie.

Two angling clubs manage large portions of this river — the Dalbeattie and the Castle Douglas Angling Associations — and they do it very well. The latter has seven miles of water. Both clubs annually stock the river with brown trout and they welcome anglers to the district.

In the heart of the southern Highlands

An excellent Solway water (Cree)

Do not look under 'L' in the fishing guide guidebooks for that excellent little river the Luce away down in the far south-west, because there are really *two* rivers — the Cross Water of Luce and the Main Water of Luce. They meet at New Luce in the heart of West Galloway, surrounded by moorland and hill place-names that are poetry in themselves — Cairnscarrow . . . Craig Fel . . . Gleniron Fell.

The Water of Luce rises in the moorlands of Ayrshire and the course of much of the river can be seen from the train on the main railway line between Girvan and Stranraer. When it leaves New Luce it runs at a good flow for six miles to the sea at Luce Sands fringing Luce Bay. It really is a spate stream but in its middle and upper waters there are plenty of brown trout. The fishing just below New Luce is particularly good.

Sea trout fishing, however, takes this small river to the top of the list. No matter how good it is today for angling these fish, consider what the river produced many years ago. A Major Ashley Dodd is on record for having fished for three separate nights and for catching respectively 168, 166 and 145 sea trout. On the same river he caught forty-eight sea trout and six salmon on a 10-foot trout fly rod.

The fishing on the Luce is owned, to a large extent, by Stair Estates, but some fishing is available to visitors through the Stranraer and District Angling Association. They have the fishing in a part of the Cross Water upstream from Quarter Bridge.

The Cree is a river in the very south-west part of Scotland. It rises up in Loch Moan in south Ayrshire and west Kirkcudbrightshire then bends away to the west for some distance and works round to the south-east. Its total is twenty-six miles.

Many tourists from England, indeed too many, miss this lovely part of Scotland altogether in their hurry to get north. This area of Galloway has beautiful scenery and unspoiled, sparsely populated tracts of hill country. The main centre is Newton Stewart and permits to fish the Cree and other waters can be obtained from tackle shops or from the local hotels and caravan sites.

As a river flowing into Wigtown Bay on the Solway Firth it attracts, like the Nith, the Annan, the Bladenoch, the Dee and Fleet, thousands of salmon and sea trout from the Solway. Down at the mouth of the Cree the haaf netters are at work much of the year with their portable pock nets which they use to intercept salmon. This method of fishing needs great skill, endurance and a thorough knowledge of the depth of the channels and the tides. The Solway tides are notorious for their speed and, at times, an incoming tide will outpace a galloping horse. Thus a haaf-net victim is claimed by the sea every few years.

In the conventional sphere of rod-and-line angling on the Cree itself, there is some excellent sea trout and brown trout fishing, as well, of course, as salmon. The Newton Stewart and District Angling Association controls much of the lower reaches of the river and they encourage visiting anglers. The river has four main tributaries, the Minnoch, Trool, Penkiln and the Palnure. The Minnoch is the largest of these and goes deeper into Ayrshire than the Cree itself. The association's permits cover some miles of the main river from the suspension bridge above the town, plus a good stretch of the Palnure and Penkiln waters and two miles of the west bank of the Minnoch.

Where to get permission to fish

River	Fishing Area	Get the permit from . . .
Add	Kilmartin	Duntrune Castle, Kilmartin.
Allan	Bridge of Allan	D. Crockart & Son, 47 King Street, Stirling. Allanbank Hotel, Greenloaning. McLaren Fishing Tackle, Bridge of Allan.
Almond	Cramond	Cramond Angling Club. Post Office, Cramond. Post Office, Davidsons Mains. 'Shooting Lines' Roseburn.
Almond	West Lothian	River Almond Angling Association, Secretary, H. Meikle, 23 Glen Terrace, Deans Livingston. Tel: Livingston 411813.
Alness	—	Novar Estate Office, Evanton. Tel: 0349 830208.
Alness	—	Alness Angling Club, Mr J. B. Patterson Iron Monger, 33-35 High Street, Alness.
Alness	—	Coul House Hotel, Contin, By Strathpeffer.
Alness	—	Craigdarroch Lodge Hotel, Contin, By Strathpeffer.
Annan	Newbie Estates	Newbie Estates. Mainly time share, some daily and weekly permits available. Mrs Bailey, Newbie Mill, Annan. Tel: (04612) 2608.
Annan	Hoddam	Hoddam. Mrs C. Clark, Bridgend Cottage, Hoddam. Tel: Ecclefechan (05763) 488.
Annan	Castlemilk (St Mungo)	Castlemilk (St Mungo), Castlemilk Estate Office, Norwood, Lockerbie. Tel: Kettleholm (05765) 203.
Annan	Royal Four Towns	Castlemilk (St Mungo), Castlemilk Estate Office, Norwood, Lockerbie. Tel: Kettleholm (05765) 203.
Annan	Halieaths	Messrs McJerrow and Stevenson, Solicitors, Lockerbie. Tel: (05762) 2123.
Annan	Applegirth (Also Kinnel and Dryfe Waters)	Applegirth (including Kinnel and Dryfe waters), Mr Graham, The Smithy, Millhousebridge, Lochmaben. Tel: (038781) 397. Red House Hotel, Wamphray. Tel: Johnstonebridge (05764) 214.
Annan	Annandale Estates	St Ann's, Lockerbie. Tel: Johnstonebridge (05764) 317.
Annan	Upper Annandale Angling Assoc.	Mr J. B. Black, 1 Rosehill, Grange Road, Moffat. Tel: (0683) 20104.
Avon	1½ miles of right bank near Tomintoul	Post Office, The Square, Tomintoul AB3 9ET. Tel: Tomintoul (08074) 201.
Avon	North of Tomintoul	Richmond Arms Hotel, The Square, Tomintoul, AB3 9ET. Tel: Tomintoul (08074) 209.
Avon	Last six miles before Confluence with Spey	Estate Office, Ballindalloch AB3 9AX. Tel: Ballindalloch (08072) 205.
Awe	Taynuilt	Inverawe/Taynuilt Fisheries, Argyll. Tel: (08662) 262.
Awe	Muchairn Beat — Red Bank to Grey Pool	Nelson, Muchairn. Tel: 92241.
Awe	Barrage Beat — South Bank	Bell Ingram, Edinburgh. Tel: 073 821121.

River	Fishing Area	Get the permit from . . .
Ayr	Ayr	Director of Finance, Kyle and Carrick District Council, Town Buildings, Ayr. James Kirk, Union Arcade, Ayr. Gamesport, 60 Sandgate, Ayr.
	Mauchline	Mauchline Ballochmyle Angling Club, per J. F. McCall, Post Office, High Street, Mauchline.
	Auchinleck	Auchinleck Angling Association, per J. McColm, 21 Milne Avenue, Auchinleck.
Berriedale	All	The Factor, Welbeck Estates Office, Berriedale. Tel: Berriedale 237.
Blackwater	Above Rogie Falls.	Mr Burr, Spar Shop, Strathpeffer. Tel: 0997 21561 or 21876. East Lodge Hotel, Strathconon. Tel: 0997 7222.
Blackwater	Middle Beat	Craigdarroch Lodge Hotel, Contin, By Strathpeffer. Tel: 0997 21265.
Blackwater	Lower Beat	Craigdarroch Lodge Hotel, Contin, By Strathpeffer. Tel: 0997 21265.
Bladenoch	—	Mr Peter McDougall, Corsemalzie House Hotel, Portwilliam. Tel: Mochrum (098886) 254. Tarff Hotel, Kirkcowan. Tel: (067183) 325.
Border Esk	—	Esk & Liddle Fisheries Association. Mr J. B. Hill, c/o Messrs Stevenson and Johnstone, Langholm. Tel: (0541) 80428. Eskdale Hotel, Langholm. Tel: (0541) 264. Bailiff. Tel: Canonbie (05415) 279.
Clyde	Kirkfieldbank to Easter Sils Farm (7 miles)	Controlled by: Lanark & District Angling Associaton. Permits: Taid Flies & Fishing Tackle, 75 Wellgate, Lanark. Tel: (0555) 2302.
Clyde	Thankerton-Roberton (10 miles)	Controlled by: Lamington & District Angling Association. Permits: Mr B. F. Dexter, 18 Boghall Park, Biggar. Tel: (0899) 20577. or Messrs Bryden, 153 High Street, Biggar. Tel: (0899) 20069.
Clyde	Main river from The Source to Motherwell (40 miles)	Controlled by: United Clyde Angling Protective Association. Permits: Mr J. Quigley, 39 Hillfoot Avenue, Coltness, Cambusnethan. Tel: (0698) 382479 and Tackle Shops.
Conon	Above Loch Achonachie	Mr Burr, Spar Shop. Strathpeffer. Tel: 0997 21561 or 21876. East Lodge Hotel, Strathconon. Tel: 0997 7222.
Conon	Bahan Beats	Coul House Hotel, Contin, By Strathpeffer.
Conon	Lower Beat-Conon railway Bridge to the sea	Dingwall Angling Club. The Sports and Model Shop, Tulloch Street, Dingwall. Tel: 0349 62346.
Conon	Middle and Lower Bahan Beats	Highland Estate, Brahan, By Dingwall. Tel: 0349 61150.
Cree	Upper Reaches	Commercial Hotel, Barrhill, Ayrshire. Tel: (046582) 244.
Cree	Newton Stewart	Newton Stewart Angling Association water. The Gun Shop, Newton Stewart. Tel: (0671) 2570. Time share terms from G. M. Thomson and Co. 10 Victoria Street, Newton Stewart. Tel: (0671) 2887. Occasional two-day permits.

River	Fishing Area	Get the permit from . . .
Cross Water of Luce	New Luce	Stranraer and District Angling Association. McDiarmid Sports Shop. 90 George Street. Stranraer. Tel: (0776) 2705 and local hotels.
Deveron	Right hand bank between the Turriff Burn and the Deveron Bridge adjacent to Turriff Sewage Works	Ian Masson Fishing Tackle, 6 Castle Street, Turriff.
Deveron	Huntly Lodge	Bell Ingram, Durn, Isla Road, Perth. Tel: Perth (0738) 21121.
Deveron	River Deveron — Upper Netherdale — 2 miles of left bank opposite Inverkeithny	Drummuir Estate Office, Drummuir, Keith AB5 3JE. Tel: Drummuir (054281) 225.
Deveron	Banff	L. Smith (River Bailiff), 52 Berrymuir Road, Macduff. Tel: Macduff (0261) 33466.
Deveron	By Huntly	J. Christie Esq. 27 Duke Street, Huntly. Tel: Huntly (0466) 2291. G. Manson, Sports Shop, 45 Gordon Street, Huntly. Tel: Huntly (0466) 2482.
Deveron	Adjacent to Castle Hotel, Huntly	Castle Hotel, Huntly.
Deveron	Various Beats from Huntly to near Turriff	G. Manson, 45 Gordon Street, Huntly. Tel: Huntly (0466) 2482.
Deveron	Turriff (West bank from junction of Muiresk Water to Deveron Bridge. Both banks from bridge to point opposite Knockie Mill)	Ian Masson Fishing Tackle, 6 Castle Street, Turriff. Tel: Turriff (0888) 62428.
Deveron	Beldorney Castle	Bell Ingram, Durn, Isla Road, Perth. Tel: Perth (07328) 21121.
Devon	Dollar	Devon Angling Association. R. Breingan, 33 Redwell Place, Alloa. Tel: Alloa 215185. Scobble Sports, Primrose Street, Alloa. D. W. Black, Hobby shop, 10 New Row, Dunfermline. D. Crockart & Son, 47 King Street, Stirling. Tel: (0786) 73443.
Doon	Patna	Drumgrange and Keirs Angling Club, per Palace Bar, Dalmellington Road, Waterside. Tel: Patna (0292) 531204.
	Skeldon	Mrs C. Henderson, Skeldon Caravan Park, Hollybush by Ayr. Tel: (0292) 56580. (Private Fishing).
	Skeldon	Mrs Campbell, Skeldon Mains, Dalrymple, Ayr. Tel: (0292) 56656. (Fishing breaks)
Don	Glenkindie	Glenkindie Arms Hotel, Glenkindie, Strathdon. Tel: Glenkindie (097 53) 288. Salmon £6 per day. Trout £3.50 per day.
Don	Kintore 2½ miles on Right Bank 3½ miles on Left Bank	Kintore Arms Hotel, Kintore. Tel: Kintore (0467) 32216. J. Copland, Newsagent, 2 Northern Road, Kintore. Tel: Kintore (0467) 32210. (Open 6.30 am-5.30 pm) Post Office, 1 Northern Road, Kintore. Tel: Kintore (0467) 32201. Hillhead Caravan Park, Kintore. Tel: Kintore (0467) 32809. (Open daily)

149

Where to get permission to fish

River	Fishing Area	Get the permit from . . .
Don	Kildrummy 4 miles by Glenkindie	Mr T. Hillary, Auchnavenie, Kildrummy, Nr Alford. Tel: Kildrummy (03365) 208.
Don	Alford	Forbes Arms Hotel, Bridge of Alford. Tel: Alford (0336) 2108.
Don	Glenkindie 2¼ miles	Bell Ingram, Durn, Isla Road, Perth. Tel: Perth (0738) 21121.
Don	Bridge of Kemnay to the Old Mill	Mrs Milton, Kemnay House, Kemnay.
Don	Upper Parkhill by Dyce and Lower Parkhill	Jas Somers & Son, 40 Thistle Street, Aberdeen. Tel: Aberdeen (0224) 639910.
Don	Forbes Estate	Forbes Estate, Estate Office, Whitehouse, By Alford. Tel: Alford (0336) 2524. The majority of fishing is booked by the week in advance.
Don	Upper Fintray	Jas Somers & Son, 40 Thistle Street, Aberdeen. Tel: Aberdeen (0224) 639910.
Don	Monymusk	Grant Arms Hotel, Monymusk. Tel: Monymusk (046 77) 226.
Don	By Inverurie 2 miles Polinar Burn downstream to junction of River Urie on North Bank	J. Duncan, 4 West High Street, Inverurie. Tel: Inverurie (0467) 20310. P. McPherson, Ironmonger, 49 Market Place, Inverurie. Tel: Inverurie (0467) 21363. Hillhead Caravan Park, Kintore. Tel: Kintore (0467) 32809. (Open daily) (This permit also applies to fishing on River Urie).
Don	Manar Beat situated immediately above Burgh Water approx: 1.6 miles	J. Duncan, 4 West High Street, Inverurie. Tel: Inverurie (0467) 20310.
Don	8 miles South Bank between Lub Bridge and Bridge of Newe	Colquhonnie Hotel, Strathdon. Tel: Strathdon (097 52) 210.
Don	Tamashean Water 2 miles	Mr McIntosh, Donview, Strathdon.
Don	Towie	Strutt & Parker, 68 Station Road, Banchory AB3 3YJ. Tel: Banchory (03302) 4888. Mr W. Robertson, Balronald, Tillypronie, Tarland. Tel: Tarland (03391) 332.
Don	Various Beats	Macsport Ltd, Macsport House, Ballater Road, Aboyne. Tel: Aboyne 2896.
Earn	Forteviot (Broomhill)	David Black, Hobby & Model Shop, New Row, Dunfermline. Tel: Dunfermline 22582.
Earn	(Very small Beat)	Earnbank House Hotel, Bridge of Earn, Perthshire. Tel: Bridge of Earn 812360.
Earn	Private Beat	Royal Hotel, Comrie, Perthshire. Tel: Comrie 70200.
Earn	Association Waters	W. Cook & Son, High Street, Crieff, Perthshire. Tel: Crieff 2081. St Fillans & Loch Earn Angling Association. J. Macpherson Rannoch, 4 Earn View, St Fillians, Perthshire. Tel: St Filians 219.
Elvan	All	Controlled by: United Clyde Angling Protective Association. Permits: Mr J. Quigley, 39 Hillfoot Avenue, Coltness, Cambusnethen. Tel: (0698) 382479.

River	Fishing Area	Get the permit from . . .
Endrick	Drymen	Loch Lomond Improvement Association, per R. A. Clements CA, 29 St Vincent Street, Glasgow. Tel: 041-221 0068. (Members only)
Esk	Musselburgh	Musselburgh and District Angling Association. T. Mealyou, Sports Shop, 11 Newbiggin, Musselburgh. NO SUNDAY FISHING. Regulations on permit.
Esk	Midlothian	Esk Valley Angling Improvement Association. Kevin Burns, 53 Fernieside Crescent, Edinburgh. Tel: 031 664 4685. Local shops. Officials on water. Fly Rod and Reel ONLY to be used. Regulations on permit. Sunday Fishing.
Findhorn	Near Forres	The Tackle Shop, 97b High Street, Forres IV36 0AA. Tel: Forres (0309) 72936.
Fleet	Gatehouse-of-Fleet	Rusko and Cally Estates. Murray Arms Hotel. Gatehouse-of-Fleet. Tel: (05574) 207. Murray Arms Hotel, Gatehouse of Fleet.
Forth	Stirling	Stirling District Council, Admin & Legal Dept., Municipal Buildings, Corn Exchange, Stirling. Tel: (0786) 79000. D. Corckart & Son, 47 King Street, Stirling. Tel: (0786) 73443. McLarens, 4 Allanvale, Bridge of Allan. Tel: (0786) 833530. Guns & Ammo, 5 Friars Street, Stirling. Tel: (0786) 62182.
Garnock	Dalry	Dalry Garnock AC per G. King, 8 Peden Avenue, Dalry. David Morton's Newsagent, Main Street, Dalry.
	Kilwinning	Kilwinning Eglinton AC, per M. Tudhope, 15 Viaduct Circle, Kilwinning. Water Bailiffs and local shops.
	Kilbirnie	Kilbirnie Angling Club, Johnstone, 93 Dalry Road, Kilbirnie.
Girvan	Girvan	Carrick Angling Club, per T. L. Wilson, 1 Church Square, Girvan.
Irvine	Irvine	Irvine and District AC, per A. Sim, 5-1 Ruby Crescent. Irvine Currie Sports, 32 High Street, Irvine. Tel: Irvine (2094) 78603. Dreghorn AC per M. Fullarton, 12 Rigfoot, Girdle Toil, Irvine. Allison's Florists, Bank Street, Irvine.
	Kilmarnock	Kilmarnock AC per McCuricks, 39 John Finnie Street, Kilmarnock.
	Galston	Galston AC per J. Steven, 12 Millands Road, Galston. Valley Sports, Galston. Tel: Galston (0563) 821747.
	Hurlford	Hurlford and Crookedholm AC per Hurlford Post Office. The Thack Inn, Hurlford. Tel: Kilmarnock (0563) 22914. P. and R. Torbet, 27 Portland Street, Kilmarnock. Tel: (0563) 41734.
	Darvel	Darvel AC per E. Slaven, 18 Armour Terrace, Darvel. Tel: Darvel (0560) 21551.
	Newmilns	Newmilns Angling Club, per Stupparts Newsagent.
Isla	Grange	No permit required.

Where to get permission to fish

River	Fishing Area	Get the permit from . . .
Isla	The right bank from the Haughs of Cairnie to its junction with the Deveron	J. Christie Esq., 27 Duke Street, Huntly. Tel: Huntly (0466) 2291 also Mr G. Manson, 45 Gordon Street, Huntly. Tel: Huntly (0466) 2482.
Leven	All	Loch Lomond Angling Improvement Association. c/o R. A. Clement & Co CA 29 St Vincent Place, Glasgow G1 1HH. Tel: 041-221-0068.
Leven	Barloch — Dumbarton	Loch Lomond Angling Improvement Association, per Messrs R. A. Clements CA, 29 St Vincent Street, Glasgow. Tel: 041-221 0068. Local Tackle Shops.
Livet	Glenlivet	Richmond Arms Hotel, The Square, Tomintoul AB3 9ET. Tel: Tomintoul (08074) 209.
Machrie	Arran	Strathtay Estate Office, Aberfeldy, Perthshire. Tel: (0887) 20496.
Moriston	Torgyle to River Mouth	Glenmoriston Estate Office, Glenmoriston, Nr Inverness. Tel: Glenmoriston 51202.
Naver	Bettyhill	Bettyhill Hotel, Bettyhill, Sutherland. Tel: Bettyhill 202.
Ness	All	Inverness Angling Club Secretary, G. M. Smith, 50 Nevis Park, Inverness. Tel: 238197. Grahams, 71 Castle Street, Inverness, Tel: 233178. M. Jamieson, Fishing Tackle, 58 Church Street, Inverness. Tel: 239199. Also available from the Tourist Information Centre.
Nith	Dumfries	Director of Finance, Nithsdale District Council, Municipal Chambers, Dumfries. Tel: Dumfries 53166.
Nith	Dumfries	Dumfries and Galloway Angling Association. Secretary D. G. Conchie, 46 Barrie Avenue, Cresswell, Dumfries. Tel: 55223. D McMillan, 6 Friar's Vennel, Dumfries.
Nith	Thornhill	Mid-Nithsdale Angling Association. Pollack & Oag, 1 West Morton Street, Thornhill.
Nith	Thornhill	Buccleuch Estates Ltd. Drumlanrig Mains, Thornhill. Tel: (08486) 283.
Nith	Sanquhar	Upper Nithsdale Angling Association, W. Forsyth, Solicitor, 100 High Street, Sanquhar, Dumfries-shire. Tel: Sanquhar 241.
Nith	New Cumnock	New Cumnock Angling Association. A. Lockhart, 79 Dalhanna Drive, New Cumnock.
North Esk	Cawterland — Gallery	Joseph Johnson & Sons Ltd. 3 America Street, Montrose. Tel: Montrose 72666.
North Esk	Murphie. Upstream of A92 Bridge	As above.
North Esk	Gallery — Hatton	Links Hotel, Montrose. Tel: Montrose 72288.
Polly	Ullapool	Mrs A. McLeod, Inverpolly, Ullapool, Ross-shire. Tel: Lochinver 482.
Spey	Various Private Beats	Dowans Hotel, Aberlour AB3 9LS. Tel: Aberlour (03405) 488. Hotel residents only. Advance booking required.

River	Fishing Area	Get the permit from . . .
Spey	Aberlour	J. A. J. Munro, 95 High Street, Aberlour AB3 9PB. Tel: Aberlour (03405) 428. Visitors' permits available to visitors staying overnight in Aberlour. Not bookable in advance. First fish caught may be kept by angler, all other fish caught on the same day to be handed in to J. A. J. Munro for sale for the good of the village. Beat 2: Bag limit of 2 fish per day, second fish to be handed in as above.
Spey	Orton Water South of Fochabers	Orton Management Co. Ltd, Estate Office Orton, Fochabers IV32 7QE. Tel: Orton (034388) 240. Available only to guests resident in Estate Lodges (self-catering cottages also available).
Spey	Fochabers	Speyside Heating, Plumbing & Electrical Ltd, 91 High Street, Fochabers IV32 7DH. Tel: (0343) 820531.
Spey	Craigellachie	Enquiries to Mr W. Roy Craigmichael, Maggieknockater. Tel: Craigellachie (03404) 387.
Spey	Spey Dam to below Kingussie	The Paper Shop, Kingussie Street, Newtonmore. Tel: 05403 242 and A. L. Donald, Ironmongers.
Spey	North Side, Kincraig Bridge to Forestry Plantation by Eilein Burn	Alvie Estate Office, Kincraig. Tel: 05404 255 and Dalraddy Caravan Park, Near Aviemore.
Spey	Inverdruie	Rothiemurch Fishing Centre, Inverdurie by Aviemore. Tel: 0479 810703.
Spey	Left Bank from Spey Road Bridge to Dalfaber Burn	The Osprey Fishing School, Shopping Precinct, Aviemore. Tel: 0479 810132 or 810911.
Spey	Miller's Pool to Broomhill Pool	Ben O Gar Stores, Boat of Garten. Tel: 0479 83 372 and at hotel reception for residents of the Boat Hotel and Craigard Hotel, Boat of Garten and Nethybridge Hotel, Nethybridge. Permits are only available to visitors booking overnight accommodation in either Boat of Garten, Carrbridge, Dulnain Bridge or Nethybridge.
Spey	Both Banks for 7 miles from Broomhill Bridge to 1 mile below Grantown Old Bridge	Grant Mortimer, High Street, Grantown. Tel: 0479 2684.
South Esk	Kirriemuir (6 miles)	Kirriemuir Angling Club, 13 Lova Road, Kirriemuir. Tel: Kirriemuir 73456. Dykehead Post Office.
Stinchar	Colmonell	Boars Head Hotel, Colmonell. Tel: (046588) 272. Queen's Hotel, Colmonell.
Tay	Private Beat	Clova Hotel, Glen Clova, Angus. Tel: Clova 222.
Tay	Ballinluig	Logierait Pine Lodges, Ballinluig. Tel: Ballinluig 253.
Tay	Aberfeldy (2½ miles)	Jamieson's Sports Shop, Dunkeld Street, Aberfeldy. Tel: Aberfeldy 20385.
Tay	Ballathie Beat	Estate Office, Ballathie Farms, Balmains, Stanley, Perthshire. Tel: Meikleour 250.
Tay	Derculich Beat	Finlayson Hughes, Estate Office, Aberfeldy. Tel: Aberfeldy 20234.
Tay	Grandtully (Lower)	As above.
Tay	Private Beats	Hunters Lodge, Bankfoot, Perthshire. Tel: Bankfoot 325.
Tay	Dunkeld (2 Beats Upper and Lower)	Stakis Dunkeld House Hotel, Dunkeld, Perthshire. Tel: Dunkeld 243.

Where to get permission to fish

River	Fishing Area	Get the permit from . . .
Tay	Esturial Water	City of Dundee District Council, Parks & Recreation Department, 353 Clepington Road, Dundee. Tel: Dundee 23141.
Tay	Dunkeld (2 miles) On the main A9 opposite Stakis Dunkeld House Hotel	R. Scott Miller, The 'Top Shop' Tackle Shop, Atholl Street, Dunkeld. Tel: Dunkeld 556.
Tay	City of Perth Fishings	Director of Finance, Perth & Kinross District Council, 1 High Street, Perth. Tel: Perth 39911.
Tay	Dalguise Beats	Perth & District Anglers Association, c/o Bob Sime, 57 South Methven Street, Perth. Tel: Perth 23925.
Teviot	North side: Ormiston March to Trevor Bridge. South side: Teviot Bridge to the junction	Kelso Angling Association. C Hutchison, 53 Abbotseat. J. Dickson & Son, 35 The Square. Sportswise, 43 The Square. Border Temperance Hotel, Springwood Caravan Park. Tweedside Tackle, Woodmarket.
Teviot	1 mile: Eckford (Buccleuch Estate Waters)	Mr A. Graham, Loch Keeper, The Cottage, Eckford. Tel: Crailing 255.
Teviot	2½ miles Oxnam Mouth — Nine Wells, both banks in places. 1½ miles Chesters Estate Boundary – A68 Road Bridge Cleikemin South bank only	J. T. Renilson, 4 Conangate, Jedburgh. Game and Country Enterprises. 6/8 Canongate. W. Shaw, Canongate, Jedburgh.
Teviot	including tributaries — Ale, Borthwick, Rule and Slitrig	Stotharts, 6 High Street, Pet Shop. 1 Union Street. Club Premises, 5 Sandbed. Teviotdale Lodge Hotel or Hawick A.C. Secretary.
Teviot	From Martin's Bridge on B711 to top of Chesters	Stotharts, Tackle Shop, 6 High Street, Hawick. Tel: 72331. Applications for season tickets to Hawick A.C. Secretary.
Teith	Callander Town Water	James Bain, Fishing Tackle, 76 Main Street, Callander. Tel: (0877) 30218. D Crockart & Son, 47 King Street, Stirling. Tel: (0786) 73443
	Estate Water Blue Banks	As above.
Tweed	Peebleshire Stanhope-Thornilee excl. Burgh Water and certain private stretches	Peebleshire Trout Fishing Assoc: D. G. Fyle, 39 High Street, Peebles, Tel: 20131. Stobo Countryside Centre, Stobo, I. Fraser, Tackle Dealer, High Street, Peebles. Tweed Valley Hotel, Walkerburn. Tel: 220 Sonnys Sportshop, 29 High Street, Innerleithen. John Dickson & Son, 21 Frederick Street, Edinburgh. F. & D. Simpson, 28 West Preston Street, Edinburgh. Crook Inn, Tweedsmuir.
Tweed	Peebles Area	Peebles Angling School, 10 Dean Park, Peebles. Tel: (0721) 20331.
Tweed	Traquair	J. H. Leeming ARICS, Chartered Surveyors, Stichill House, Kelso. Tel: Stichill (05737) 280. 24 hr answering service.
Tweed	Walkerburn & Innerleithen 5 miles from Holylee to Innerleithen	Tweed Valley Hotel, Walkerburn, Tel: 089687 636. Telex 940 133 44 Ref: TWEE G
Tweed	Fairnlee 3½ miles	As above.
Tweed	West Water	As above.
Tweed	Fairnlee	J. H. Leeming ARICS, Chartered Surveyors, Stitchill House, Kelso, Roxburghshire. Tel: Stitchill (05737) 280. 24 hr answering service.

River	Fishing Area	Get the permit from . . .
Tweed	8 miles from Holylee to limit notice above Ellwyn Water. (Permits at hotel)	Tweed Valley Hotel, Walkerburn. Tel: 089687 636. Telex 940 133 44 Ref: TWEE G
Tweed	Nest Beat N. Bank Caddonfoot Church upstream to Tweeddale District Boundary. (Permits at hotel)	Tweed Valley Hotel, Walkerburn. Tel: (089687) 636. Telex 940 133 44 Ref: TWEE G.
Tweed	Galashiels S. Bank Thornielee to junction of Tweed & Elwyn Burn. N. Bank Caddonfoot to junction of Tweed & Elwyn Burn – 12 miles	Gala Angling Associaton. S. Grybowski. 3 St Andrew Street, Galashiels. Tel: 56712. Messrs J. & A. Turnbull, 30 Bank Street, Galashiels. Tel: 3191. Anglers Choice, High Street, Melrose. Tel: 3070. Thornilee House Hotel, Clovenfords. Tel: 350. Kingsknowes Hotel, Galashiels. Tel: 3478. Clovenfords Hotel, Clovenfords. Tel: 203.
Tweed	Tweed/Ettrick Galashiels Sunderland Hall	R. Smyly, Sunderland Hall, Galashiels. Tel: Selkirk 21293.
Tweed	Lowood Bridge, Nr Melrose Right Bank	Mr L. B. Smith, Darnlee, Darnick, Melrose. Tel: 2261.
Tweed	Melrose ½ mile North Bank, from suspension bridge to end of the haugh at Friar's Hall: South Bank from upper limit St Helens water downstream to Mill Lade Newstead	Melrose & District Angling Association. Anglers Choice, High Street, Melrose. Tel: 3070. T. McLeish, Planetree Cottage, Newstead, Melrose. Tel: Melrose 2232.
Tweed	Melrose St Aidens, Gattonside House to Suspension Bridge	The Brother Superior, St Aidens. Gattonside.
Tweed	Melrose (Ravenswood & Tweedswood)	Anglers Choice, High Street, Melrose.
Tweed	Melrose 2 miles: Pavillion to Tweedswood Old Leaderfoot Bridge to Leader	As above.
Tweed	Newtown. St Boswells, S. Bank: Monksford - Littledean. N. Bank: Dryburgh - Dallove Burn other than where marked private	Mr Law, Main Street, St Boswells. C. D. Grant, Newsagent, Newtown St Boswells. Buccleuch Hotel, St Boswells. Mr E. Cockburn, Fishermans House, Dryburgh. Dryburgh Abbey Hotel. Anglers Choice, Melrose. Miss A Laing, Newsagent, Newtown St Boswells.
Tweed	St Boswells. 3 miles.	Dryburgh Abbey Hotel, St Boswells. Tel: 0835 22261.
Tweed	Kelso S. Side: Junction Pool to Kelso Bridge and Mellendean Burn to top of Broase St. (except private water)	Kelso Angling Association. C. Hutchison, 53 Abbotseat. J. Dickson & Son, 35 The Square. Sportswise, 43 The Square. River Watchers. Border Temperance Hotel. Springwood Caravan Park. Tweedside Tackle. Woodmarket.
Tweed	Birgham Dub	Douglas & Angus Estates, per The Hon. Caroline Douglas-Home, The Hirsel, Coldstream.
Tweed	The Lees (Coldstream)	J. H. Leeming ARICS, Chartered Surveyor, Stichill House, Kelso. Tel: Stichill (0573) 280. 24 hr Answering Service.

River	Fishing Area	Get the permit from . . .
Tweed	Lennel Beat Birgham Wark and Lees Beats	Tweed Fishing Tackle, Market Street, Coldstream. Tel: 2719.
	Coldstream (Town Waters)	Crown Hotel, Market Sq., Coldstream. Tel: 2558.
Tweed	Cornhill. 4 miles Coldstream Bridge to Dreeper Island	Tillmouth Park Hotel. Tel: Coldstream 2255.
Tweed	Milne Graden	The Manager, Milne Graden, Coldstream.
Tweed	Ladykirk Norham Bridge Horncliffe	Ladykirk and Norham Angling Association, Masons Arms, Norham. Tel: (0289) 82237.
Tweed	Ladykirk (Norham)	J. H. Leeming Chartered Surveyor, Stichill House, Kelso. Tel: Stichill (05737) 280. 24 hr Answering Service.
Tweed	Norham Dean Burn at West Newbiggan	Farm House, Newbiggin, Norham.
Tweed	Horncliffe Tidal waters to Berwick	N/A (FREE).
Tummel	Port-na-Craig suspension bridge to Ballinluig (north bank) and just below Milton of Fonab Caravan Site to Ballinluig (south bank)	Pitlochry Tourist Information Centre, Atholl Road, Pitlochry. Peter D. Malloch (Sports Shop), Atholl Road, Pitlochry. Ballinluig Post Office.
Tummel	From Pitlochry Dam to bottom of Milton of Fonab Caravan Site (south bank)	Ross Gardiner. Tel: Pitlochry 2157 (evenings)
Tummel	Ballinluig	Logierait Pine Lodges, Ballinluig. Tel: Ballinluig 253.
Ugie	Pitfour Fishings	Dicks Sports, 54 Broad Street, Fraserburgh or G. Milne Esq, Newsagent, 3 Ugie Road, Peterhead. Tel: 72584.
Ugie	1 mile North of Peterhead extending Westwards	As above.
Ugie	At Old Deer (From bridge on B9030 on the North side of Old Deer to bridge on the South side of Old Deer).	Rangers Office, Aden Country Park, Old Deer. Tel: (0771) 22857.
Water of Leith	Edinburgh	Lothian Regional Council Reception, George IV Bridge, Edinburgh. Tel: 031 229 9292 ext: 2355. Post Office, Balamo. Post Office, Currie. Post Office, Juniper Green.
Wick	All	Camp Sports Centre, High Street, Wick. David Calder, Secretary, Wick Angling Association, 13 Dunnet Avenue, Wick.
Whiteadder & Dye Tributaries	Whiteadder from source to Ninewells. (Chirnside) excl. private stretches. Dye: from confluence with Whiteadder to Byrecleugh-Horsecupcleugh March, excl. private stretches. See permit for details	Whiteadder Angling Association. D. Calder, Cranshaws J. Kerr, Hungry Snout Plough Inn, Duns. R. Welsh, Game Dealer, Castle Street, Duns. Mr Cowan, Crumstane, Duns (Bailiff). Black Bull Hotel, Duns. Red Lion Hotel, Allanton. White Swan Hotel, Duns.
Whiteadder	4½ miles private stretch Abbey St. Bathans	Abbey St. Bathans Trout Farm. Tel: (03614) 237. Head Keeper (03614) 219

River	Fishing Area	Get the permit from . . .
Whiteadder	7 miles: Canty's Bridge to Allanton Bridge excl. private stretches	Berwick & District Angling Association. D. Cowan (Hon. Sec.) 23 Bridge Street, Dewars Lane. Berwick-Upon-Tweed. Bus parties limited in numbers and by prior arrangement only with Hon. Sec. Messrs Jobson, Marygate, Berwick. Messrs Game Fair, Berwick. Red Lion, Allanton. Canty's Brig Public House. Berwick Holiday Centre.
Ythan	At Fyvie (north bank 3 mile stretch between Mill of Ardlogie and Fetterletter, Woodhead, Fyvie.	Vale Hotel, Fyvie. Tel: (065 16) 376.
Ythan	Ellon	Nuchan Hotel, Ellon. Tel: Ellon (0358) 20208.
Ythan	Newburgh	Mrs Forbes, 3 Lea Cottages, Newburgh. Tel: (03586) 297.
Ythan	At Methlick (south bank from Waterloo Bridge to Tangland Bridge)	S. French & Sons (Grocers) Methlick. Tel: Methlick (065 14) 213.

Bibliography

Blakey, Robert, *The angler's guide to the rivers and lochs of Scotland*, 1854, Thomas Murray & Son.

Brown, J. Moray, *Stray sport*, 2v, 1893, Blackwood & Sons.

Calderwood, W. L., *The salmon rivers and lochs of Scotland*, 1909, Edward Arnold.

Cooper, John Ashley, *The great salmon rivers of Scotland*, 1980, Gollancz.

Coutts, James, *Game fishing, a guide to Inverness-shire*, 2nd ed., 1969, Highlands and Islands Development Board.

Haig guide to trout fishing in Britain, ed. David Barr, 1983, Willow Books, Collins.

Lamond, Henry, *Loch Lomond*, 1931, Jackson, Wylie & Co.

Lauder, Sir Thomas Dick, *Scottish rivers*, 1874, Edmonston & Douglas.

McEwan, Bill, *Angling on Lomond*, 1980, Albyn Press.

Maitland, Peter S., *The fauna of the River Endrick*, 1966, University of Glasgow.

Mills, Derek and Graesser, Neil, *Salmon rivers of Scotland*, 1981, Cassell.

Priestley, Graham, *Angling in the Lothians*, 1980, G. Priestley.

Scott, Jock, *Game fish records*, 1936, H. F. & G. Witherby Ltd.

Speirs, Duncan, *Angling in Caithness*, 1967, John Humphries.

Stoddart, Thomas Tod, *The angler's companion to the rivers and lochs of Scotland*, 1847, William Blackwood & Sons.